THE OTHER SIDE
OF SILENCE

Jerzy Peterkiewicz

THE OTHER SIDE
OF SILENCE

THE POET AT THE LIMITS OF LANGUAGE

Słowa są bez poręczy.
Words have no banisters.

London
OXFORD UNIVERSITY PRESS
NEW YORK   TORONTO
1970

ABIGAIL E. WEEKS MEMORIAL LIBRARY
UNION COLLEGE
BARBOURVILLE, KENTUCKY

Oxford University Press, Ely House, London W.1

GLASGOW NEW YORK TORONTO MELBOURNE WELLINGTON
CAPE TOWN SALISBURY IBADAN NAIROBI LUSAKA ADDIS ABABA
BOMBAY CALCUTTA MADRAS KARACHI LAHORE DACCA
KUALA LUMPUR SINGAPORE HONG KONG TOKYO

*Printed in Great Britain by
The Bowering Press, Plymouth*

In memoriam:
Antonina P.

CONTENTS

When not otherwise credited, translations are by the author, and verse is translated into prose.

CHAPTER I

ADOLESCENT INCANTATIONS

In the end there will be no Word, some of us fear. And language shall have no dominion. This premonition seems to make most bardic claims vulnerable, whether they speak of poets as unacknowledged legislators of mankind or, more modestly, put the endurance of their words above that of marble and gold. The poet's defiance of death, in particular, sounds less authoritative today, against our heightened awareness of its global threat.

No one can leap over his Shadow/Poets leap over Death.[1]

Coleridge could say this in 1802, but to us it is merely a leap of phrase. Poets do not leap over death, they stumble. When adolescent flirtation with death becomes a serious matter for the poet, it is the possible annihilation of his words that changes his early death-wish into the funeral of poetry itself.

The poet then has two alternative courses. He may offer his talent for sacrificial slaughter, hoping perhaps that, like Abraham's, his act of submission will be revoked in the last moment by Heaven, the White Goddess, or the Muse under any other guise. He may also try to go beyond poetry, into the dark, into *la noche oscura*, to the other side of silence, 'so the darkness shall be the light, and the stillness the dancing.'[2]

Rimbaud abandoned poetry at the age of twenty. This is an obvious example of the first alternative, but his sacrifice, if it was one, becomes difficult to grasp because of his very young age. Yet St. John of the Cross speaking from the other side of silence seems to puzzle us as much. We wonder why he should have consented to speak at all.[3] Underneath such examples, however, we detect some profound dissatisfaction with poetry, a dissatisfaction which seems to be inherent in the best of poetry.

[1] Coleridge, Notebooks, February–March 1802.

[2] T. S. Eliot, *East Coker*, III.

[3] He wrote the prose commentaries on his mystical poems at the request of various people. *Subida del monte Carmelo*, for example, comments on the first two stanzas of '*En una noche oscura*'.

This study will not be concerned with the crisis in modern verse, or even with what is loosely called the breakdown in communication. Its purpose is to investigate the poets' desire to die with poetry and the desire to go beyond the words, and whether this means the ultimate failure of poetry as a literary medium or whether, on the contrary, it suggests that poetry reaches the sublime when it ceases to be a medium. An investigation limited by this query need not be limited to examples from one literature: the problem is essential to the poetic condition as a whole and thus invites a comparative treatment. I shall therefore try to integrate into my critical material those facts from lesser-known literatures, such as Polish or Russian or Argentinian, which could provide new parallels for the reader of English, French, or Spanish. I hope in particular that Norwid, a Polish contemporary of Baudelaire and Hopkins, will in this way find the wider appreciation he deserves as one of the truly great European writers. His theory of silence will be examined in chapter VII. It has, in my opinion, a validity still relevant to modern aesthetics.

I am aware at the outset that no matter what I say about poetry, I am, to borrow Eliot's phrase, making 'a raid on the inarticulate/With shabby equipment always deteriorating/In the general mess of imprecision of feeling.'[1]

I

In adolescence every poet aspires, like Rimbaud, to be '*le suprême savant*', and only too often his words sound as if he already were, the knowledge being his by verbal privilege, before the test of experience. One can understand why out of his violent innocence Rimbaud wanted to speed up the arrival of experience by forcing the gates of his private hell:[2] it was his way of honesty, a poet's honesty which none of his adolescent successors could quite emulate, either by going through hell in a hurry or by pushing untested knowledge down the throat of poetry.

In his first volume of verse, for example, the juvenile Dylan Thomas could imply that he had the secret of existence within his grasp.

[1] *East Coker*, V.
[2] *Une Saison en Enfer* stands out as his typical title.

Then all the matter of the living air
Raised up a voice, and, climbing on the words,
I spelt my vision with a hand and hair,
How light the sleeping on this soily star,
How deep the waking in the worlded clouds.[1]

Allowing for the difference in time, language, and tone, Rimbaud's tobacco-covered heart and Bacchanalian hiccoughs,[2] his idle youth '*à tout asservie*'[3] are firm enough phrases, each directly hit by impatient and self-disgusted honesty: in poem after poem they seem suspended like boulders and ready to destroy the genius who lifted them up. Yet even his precise prose pieces like '*Mauvais sang*' remain talkative in the adolescent manner. No doubt the traditional rhetoric of French verse justifies Rimbaud's fondness for exclamations, but, in fact, he has no room for silence. In this alone he betrays his youthful need for loud utterance. His occult conjuring of words in search of the Sesame-word which would open the hidden riches, all his poetic alchemy of incantations, would not allow him to stop confessing, praying, and denouncing. When the pause came, it had to be final and in its sudden finality almost hostile to any notion of creative silence.

The magicians like Rimbaud or Dylan Thomas resemble the revolutionaries for whom rhetorical incantation has similar uses. Words must act on themselves, the instant magic lies in the very utterance. That is why a propagandist like Mayakovsky can shout the facts down, believing that what he invokes for the communist future has already become a fact by virtue of being uttered.

I feel
    I'm a Soviet factory,
manufacturing happiness.
I don't want to be a wayside flower,
plucked after work in an idle hour.
I want State Plan to sweat in debate
assigning my output as part of the State.[4]

The curious thing about the revolutionary type of incanta-

---

[1] 'I fellowed sleep', from *18 Poems* (London, 1934).

[2] '*Le Coeur volé*' (The stolen heart).

[3] '*Chanson de la plus haute tour*' (Song of the highest tower).

[4] '*Domoi*' (Homewards), translated by Herbert Marshall in *Mayakovsky and his Poetry* (Bombay, 1955).

tion is that it should be so dependent on the concept of the
'*suprême savant*' within the poet. Because of this the early bards
of the Russian revolution spoke with a remarkable honesty,
which the countless imitators of Mayakovsky could not attain,
thirty years later, in the new communist republics. Instead,
they faithfully adhered to the idiosyncratic typography of his
verse, breaking up the lines in Polish or Bulgarian to make
them look like the master's printed staircases. But the poet
magician of propaganda vanished with the man who in 1930,
the year he shot himself, could speak 'at the top of his voice':

> My verses stand
> > in lead-heavy letters,
> > ready for death
> > > and for deathless glory.[1]

There is a malicious portrait of Mayakovsky to be found
among Ivan Bunin's reminiscences.[2] To a sophisticated and
much older writer he appeared as a noisy *poseur*. No magic, only
pretence, and crude at that. Bunin saw him with a novelist's eye
and from a distance which was further extended by memory.
The antics of a retarded adolescent merged with the violence
of his verse which he used to recite like an actor, and the meaning of the man became bleared. It must have been hard at the
time for any observer to distinguish between the insane violence
of the revolution and the violence of a mad-looking poet.

But Mayakovsky's honesty could not have forced itself out in
any other way: his shrill voice took strength from the adolescent
fervour of a new creed. When the fervour spent itself in dogmatic
politics and bureaucracy, the poet had to become an observer
and to mature through doubt.[3] The doubt led him to a violent
end. I shall return to this in the next chapter.

Sending a revolutionary poet on tour '*pour épater le bourgeois*'
is a mid-twentieth-century improvement on the Mayakovsky
image. This happened in 1962 when Evtushenko performed his
verses while travelling through Europe and the United States.
The way in which the audiences, West German in particular,

[1] '*Vo vyes golos*' (At the top of my voice), translated by Herbert Marshall, op. cit·
[2] *Memories and Portraits* (London, 1951). Bunin and Mayakovsky are well contrasted in Valentin Katayev's memoirs, *The Grass of Oblivion* (London, 1969).
[3] The doubt was always present in his love lyrics, some of them almost tentative
in their posing of emotion, in contrast to the bravado of his political poems; e.g.
'I love', 'About this'.

responded to the young man's incantations in his native tongue which few among them understood, had little to do with the appreciation of literature, but far more with magic. Once again adolescent exhibitionism appealed to the adolescent idea of the poet, the spell-caster who can exorcise the unbearable silence within us.

Evtushenko, like Mayakovsky, is conscious of his dynamic appeal and knows how to answer those who judge his youth. 'Fear not to be young, precocious', he says in a poem, 'hurry on, if there is somewhere you can hurry.'[1] It would be irrelevant here to discuss the merits or demerits of Evtushenko's poetry: the phenomenon is interesting enough in itself as a most recent offshoot from the Mayakovsky myth.

One finds analogies with the public reception of poetry in the thirties. This decade, especially the period of the Spanish civil war, has now been re-examined critically in a number of books.[2] Committed verse tries to reach us from the past. But to make it comprehensible today, an anthologist has to illustrate not only the political beliefs of that time, but also the very nature of rhapsodic utterance which invests words with persuasive power beyond their capability. Let us take John Cornford's statement in a poem: 'Now, with my Party, I stand quite alone.' This is commitment, clear and simple. Then Cornford goes on to rhapsodize:

> Oh, be invincible as the strong sun,
> Hard as the metal of my gun . . .[3]

In lines like these the words confirm a belief, but they overreach themselves in each comparison. Their emotional validity has consequently paled with time. What remains strong is the fact of death: the poet was killed in action, and if we know this as his readers today, even a modest lyrical poem like 'Huesca' has for us the authenticity of a document. In my view, it is death which makes it mature for our time. Between the senti-

---

[1] '*S usmeshkoi o tebe inye sudyat*' (Others may judge you), translated by George Reavey in *Modern European Poetry* (New York, 1966). The last phrase is in my rendering.

[2] E.g. Hugh Ford, *A Poet's War: British Poets and the Spanish War* (London, 1966); Peter Stansky and William Abrahams, *Journey to the Frontier* (London, 1966).

[3] 'Full Moon at Tierz' in *Poems for Spain*, edited by Stephen Spender and John Lehmann (London, 1939).

ment and the biographical fact there works an enduring contrast which preserves the tone of this little poem better than any
rhapsodic amplification. No contrast, however, can be found to
sharpen 'The Conflict', one of the political poems of C. Day
Lewis. The words claim too much from their potential meaning,
and are in this sense adolescent:

> And private stars fade in the blood-red dawn
> Where two worlds strive.
>
> The red advance of life
> Contracts pride, calls out the common blood. . . .[1]

Stars, worlds, life, pride, blood: no qualifying adjective can
here relieve the congested effect of abstractions. Preaching and
propaganda are made of such stuff. And yet Day Lewis had the
good sense to declare himself on the side of the fairy tale and
the parable when he said in an essay about 'Revolution in
Writing': 'The fairy tale, the parable will survive, I believe,
because it is a unique channel of education. Propaganda,
sermons, scientific text-books, can influence the conscious mind
only.'[2]

But what is one to do with the facts hurriedly exploited for the
sake of a legend? In his autobiography Stephen Spender shows
how reversible a fact can be in the educational channel of propaganda. The Communists, for instance, 'canonized the poet
García Lorca, who had been obligingly assassinated by the
Francoists, and whom they would have attacked as a Catholic
reactionary, had he survived'.[3] The autobiography appeared
when Spender was forty-two, a right age for looking back in
sceptical puzzlement. His generation had produced paradoxes
in both camps of commitment.

Roy Campbell, for example, believed in the Nationalist
cause. He saw the horror of the civil war, was shocked by the
acts of sacrilege and, though he did not fight for Franco, his

---

[1] From *A Time to Dance* (New York, 1936).

[2] Included in *A Time to Dance*.

[3] *World within World* (London, 1951), chapter IV. In *Talking Bronco* (1946) Roy
Campbell printed this epigram 'On the Martyrdom of F. García Lorca':

> Not only did he lose his life
> By shots assassinated:
> But with a hatchet and a knife
> Was after that—translated.

verse expressed militant passions. One of his poems is entitled
'Christ in Uniform'.

> Close at my side a girl and boy
> Fall firing, in the doorway here,
> Collapsing with a strangled cheer
> As on the very couch of joy,
> And onward through a wall of fire
> A thousand others rolled the surge. . . .[1]

'A girl and boy' are no more particular than 'a thousand others',
the poem soon collapses strangled by its own rhetoric, and the
couch of joy creaks. The personal experience of war seems to be
absent. We find it later in a work which has nothing to do with
either war or political commitment. I mean Campbell's noble
translations of St. John of the Cross, which he began in 1946.
As his wife tells us in a preface, he absorbed the atmosphere
of Toledo in the crucial year of 1936, made friends with the
Carmelite monks, one of whom, the saintly Eusebio, was soon
to be murdered. 'Through him and his death he came to understand the spirit not only of St. John, but of the Cross.'[2] This
understanding one senses now in the English versions, through
the light and the stillness, and the translator's experience of
1936 is linked to that other summer, 1577, when St. John, imprisoned in a Toledan monastery, created out of suffering his
first songs of ecstasy. There is in Roy Campbell's meeting with
the Spanish mystic a strange adventure of the spirit, and the
incantations he transmutes into English show no trace of
adolescent zeal.

Some critics in the thirties had the intelligence to see youthful
muddle in the literary involvement with politics. In Harry
Kemp's symposium *The Left Heresy in Literature and Life* (to
which Laura Riding and Robert Graves contributed), we
read:

Impatience with the apparently 'abstract' results of poetry has
driven many poets to politics. . . . The abandonment of poetry for
politics is a confession of mental youthfulness; it constitutes an
acknowledgement of failure—the failure to find immediate reality in
thought. Politics have an immediacy sustained by public attention.

[1] From *Mithraic Emblems* (London, 1936).
[2] St. John of the Cross, *Poems*, translated by Roy Campbell (Penguin Classics, 1960).

The immediacy of poetry is dateless, self-sustaining, not dependent on historical interest.[1]

Later in the same passage, poetry is described as 'the completely adult expression'.

However, it would be both unimaginative and unfair to demand from an earlier generation that it should have seen through the high-minded slogans and practised abstinence in emotions. After all, the adolescents of today may still be out-witted by their own indifference to the slogans around them, and the coolness so admirably worn may turn out to have been an undistinguished sort of uniform. The incantations of the thirties belong as much to the tradition of verse and are as vulnerable as the romantic abstractions uttered with adolescent passion by poets who had the good fortune not to outlive their style because they usually died young. Formally, the different manners of youthful writing can be better compared through incantation than through the similarities in versification or content. The ecstatic figure of speech appears sometimes elaborated into a sequence, and resembles the catalogue of names and epithets used since Homeric times in epic or dithy-rambic verse.

The adolescent makers of incantation tend, I think, to adopt this type of linkage not because they want to imitate the ancients but rather out of necessity. For it is a quick, simple, and occa-sionally an effective way of ascending the scale of any passionate feeling. Moreover, it gives a semblance of structure to what is, by virtue of violent utterance, spontaneous, loose, and often hazy.

Compare this sequence from Marinetti's French poem, '*navigation tactile*', with Auden's arrangement of numbers.

Marinetti:

> Sans fin puis à toute vitesse 2000 chiens forcent le détroit de mes jambes
> Pause. immobilité
> Apathie
> 8 lents kilomètres d'éventails de plumes.[2]

---

[1] *The Left Heresy in Literature and Life* (London, 1939), Section 5. As a parallel example of sane detachment there is Louis MacNeice's short poem 'To a Com-munist' ('. . . before you proclaim the millennium, my dear, consult the baro-meter—') in *Poems* (1935).   [2] From *I nuovi poeti futuristi* (Rome, 1925).

Auden:

> Ten thousand of the desperate marching by
> Five feet, six feet, seven feet high:
> Hitler and Mussolini in their wooing poses
> Churchill acknowledging the voter's greeting
> Roosevelt at the microphone, Van der Lubbe laughing
> And our first meeting.[1]

In Marinetti the numbers work through a scheme of dynamic contrasts. But the gesture in Auden is like that of casting a net, wide enough to catch whatever is brought by a very intense and quickly passing mood. Some items are caught, but not the mood. Only when one reads a master magician does the feeling of sympathy extend to the items conjured up at random. Rimbaud's conjuring seems to allow for items as yet to be experienced. His sequence of incantation is open to trial and peril.

> A qui me louer? Quelle bête faut-il adorer? Quelle sainte image attaque-t-on? Quels coeurs briserai-je? Quel mensonge dois-je tenir? —Dans quel sang marcher? . . .—Ah! je suis tellement délaissé que j'offre à n'importe quelle divine image des élans vers la perfection.[2]

Nowadays the young poet's groping for experience is, of course, confused by the availability of facts, by instant and constant information through radio and television, by the speed of travel—no wonder catalogues of proper names occur in modern verse, sometimes as a mere echo of the world full of noises, sometimes as an attempt to push the rubble of news back into non-existence. Indigestion of vocabulary fed on geography, advertisements, names of products: it has to be relieved by howling the whole lot into the noise outside.

> —the Japanese white metal postwar trunk gaudily flowered & headed for Fort Bragg,
> one Mexican green paper package in purple rope adorned with names for Nogales,

---

[1] From *Look, Stranger!* (London, 1936), poem **XXI**. Both *Look, Stranger!* and *The Orators* of 1932 show an obsession with names, numbers, and other factual data. Auden's catalogues have value as a record of the time, and should be left as they are, unrevised. Quite rightly, Frederick Grubb objects to Auden's practice of retouching his earlier poems, 'replacing their anarchic and rebellious features with religious faith and the sense of sin'; *A Vision of Reality* (London, 1965) 4, i. It seems unwise to graft mature experience on to adolescent incantations.

[2] *Mauvais sang* (Bad blood).

B

hundreds of radiators all at once for Eureka,
crates of Hawaiian underwear,
rolls of posters scattered over the Peninsula, nuts to Sacra-
mento,
one human eye for Napa . . .[1]

How much is there still left of the belief in magical utterance?
Has youth acquired a prerogative over other ages in casting
spells? If so, what kind of poetic discretion will come of it, when
the magical summoning of names finds no response? The age of
discretion for Rilke begins with the recognition of death growing
within us, not anonymous or impersonal, but our own. Should
then the poet invoke only this one name of death to break away
from the adolescent habit of touching the surface of things with
words?

2

Two adolescents of genius, Keats and Shelley, listened to the
growth of death within them. Keats was 'half in love with
easeful Death',[2] while Shelley saw Death as 'the veil which
those who live call life'.[3] Keats died at twenty-six, Shelley at
thirty. But Shelley's invocations to Death as his invocations to
Beauty and Love are held suspect and he has been accused of
using words for words' sake. Keats, on the other hand, is
trusted; his reputation is more secure, and the intellectual
brilliance of his letters places him closer to Coleridge than to
the man who understood his death and honoured it with an
elegy.

'The only means of strengthening one's intellect is to make up
one's mind about nothing—to let the mind be a thoroughfare
for all thoughts.'[4] After reading introspective passages like this,
one is inclined to believe that had Keats lived on, he would
have transformed his lyrical idiom and, unlike Coleridge,
profited as a poet from his developing intellect. With Shelley,
the feeling or prejudice goes the other way; had he lived on, he
would have remained the Shelley we know, an adolescent rebel

---

[1] Allen Ginsberg, *In the Baggage Room at Greyhound* (III) from *Howl and Other Poems* (San Francisco, 1959).
[2] 'Ode to a Nightingale', stanza 6.
[3] *Prometheus Unbound*, III, 3.
[4] Letter to George and Georgiana Keats, 17 September 1819.

for ever confusing passion with reason, lofty ethics with idio-syncratic personal morals. This impression, undoubtedly caused by the biographical facts, can also be supported with literary evidence. The flashes of intellect which make Shelley's pamph-lets and his essay 'A Defence of Poetry' so surprisingly fresh to read, tend at the same time to reveal the essential weakness of his argument. When, for instance, he begins to draw conclu-sions from the statement that poetry is 'the centre and circum-ference of knowledge', his apologia becomes a divine oracle and parts company with our thought. A feeling of distrust creeps in and remains.

There is, however, a mood emanating from Shelley's per-sonality which wins our immediate sympathy. It could be described as a desperate, almost suicidal wooing of the *'suprême savant'* who is the poet's psyche, neither male nor female but primordial, and only glimpsed through the distorting colours of eternity. If Shelley's place was among mankind's legislators, he first had to be acknowledged by himself.

The resentment he incites in some of his readers comes from the same source as the conviction that he is a perfect example of that primordial adolescence which stands for Romanticism itself. Adolescent energy permeates the romantic inspiration, makes its prophetic voice talk too much, and drives death into a gallop until it tramples life's 'dome of many-coloured glass'. Placed high in posthumous fame, Shelley has remained a shadowy figure outside England, a disembodied voice rather than a person.[1] Yet the humanity of Shelley is what ultimately matters, despite his narcissistic withdrawal from the objects of experience. His behaviour in marriage and friendship was both touching and ridiculous, his nature both vulnerable and in-sensitive; at his best he was a poet dazzled by great visions, at his worst a hasty improviser, blinded by his own verbiage. These features of Shelley are the ones which can be detected in the representative European Romantics: in the Spaniard Espronceda, in the Russian Lermontov, in the Pole Słowacki, in the German Novalis.

To Europe at large it was not Shelley, but Byron who symbol-ized the romantic spirit, Byron the lord poet, Byron the in-constant lover and Byron the champion of Greece. In Eastern

[1] In spite of André Maurois's popular biography, *Ariel* (1923).

Europe and South America he was particularly honoured.[1] There Byron stood for liberty, and nobody knew or cared that their romantic idol had, in fact, admired Pope and sneered at Wordsworth. The Byronic identity, like a fashion, could be worn outside: his open-neck collar, his hair style, his cloak. But Shelley, whose personal legend did not fascinate Europe in this way, shared a deeper psychic identity with a greater number of poets. He and they sublimated the adolescent energy to such a degree that it made nonsense of the four ages of man: the true poet was omniscient (*allwissend*),[2] his was the psychic continuity of youth, a primordial incantation; poems therefore were in their essence unfinished, visions always fragmentary.

If Shelley typifies the individual romantic rebel, for ever trying to unbind his Promethean psyche, the *Sturm und Drang*, a literary phenomenon of the 1770s, represents collective adolescence on the march, anarchical by intention, yet longing to express itself in one total and violent act. People like Herder, Lenz, Klinger, and the young Goethe himself, were in conflict with their own temperament as much as with society. What they had in common was their youth. At the beginning of the *Sturm und Drang*, in 1770, the respective age of these bearers of stress was: Merck—twenty-nine, Herder—twenty-six, Goethe—twenty-one, Lenz—nineteen. The youngest of them, Klinger, was only eighteen, and six years later his play *Der Wirrwarr, oder Sturm und Drang* provided the stormy decade with a name.

Roy Pascal begins his study of this literary phenomenon with

---

[1] The poetry of the Argentinian Estevan Echeverría is the most interesting example of the Byronic spirit. His narrative poem *La cautiva* (1837) bears a motto from Byron and fuses the romantic melancholy with the wild scenery of the native *pampas*. His rhetorical hymn to pain, '*Himno al dolor*', is also characteristic of the manner, particularly when he expresses an almost masochistic desire:

> Yo te provoco: —descarga
> Sobre mí con mano larga
> Tus iras: yo callaré . . .

Cf. Echeverría's volume *Rimas* (Buenos Aires, 1837).

Another poet, José Mármol, reproduced the essential mood of *Childe Harold* in *El peregrino* (1847). The Polish cult of Byron was certainly intensified by life in exile, which most Polish Romantics had to accept. On the Byronic influence in Eastern Europe see M. Zdziechowski's survey, *Byron i jego wiek* (Cracow, 1897), which, in spite of its early date, is still very useful.

[2] According to the German Romantic, Novalis, '*Der echte Dichter ist allwissend; er ist eine wirkliche Welt im kleinen*' (*Fragmente*, edited by E. Kamnitzer, Dresden, 1929).

a penetrating chapter on the personalities.[1] He is right to emphasize them, for the *Sturm und Drang* was not an organized group. Each writer tried to assert himself in a different way: Merck ended in suicide, Klinger as a successful general in the Russian army. The dramatic form suited the mood of the *Sturm und Drang*: it could be battered upon by the talkative and angry heroes who were not supposed to arrive at the still point of tragedy. Klinger wrote his plays hurriedly, and the characters hurried with him, declaiming their frustrations, punctuating their speeches with exclamation marks. The inner stress and discord found its best symbol in the twins *Die Zwillinge* (1776): one has to murder the other, action can only mean violence.

It is not surprising that the early plays of Goethe and Schiller bear a similar mark of violence. The hero of *Götz von Berlichingen* (1773) is a noble knight turned rebel for whom the world, like Hamlet's Denmark, is a prison ('*Die Welt ist ein Gefängniss*', his wife says at the end of the drama); Schiller's Karl Moor in *Die Räuber* (1781) is a noble robber defying the oppressive laws of society.

At the age of twenty-eight Klinger became a professional soldier. Soon the *Geniezeit*, the time of genius and of youth triumphant, was to find its embodiment in Napoleon Bonaparte who recognized only one privilege, that of genius, and acted on it through violence. Napoleon was born in 1769, at the beginning of the *Sturm und Drang* revolt in literature. His legend haunted nineteenth-century Romanticism which, in spite of its medieval revivalism and the Herderian search after folksongs, was obsessed with topicality and the latter-day heroes. Mickiewicz, the Polish Romantic, saw in his boyhood the last glow of Napoleon's legend when his armies marched through Lithuania in 1812; he remained faithful to his hero while in exile and preached his gospel at the Collège de France until he was relieved of his post by the embarrassed authorities.

Mickiewicz and the younger Polish Romantics used the drama to express the tension of their generation, which burst out in the November rising of 1830. Part III of Mickiewicz *Dziady* (The Ancestors, 1834)[2] is set in prison, his Konrad is both a victim of

[1] *The German* Sturm und Drang (Manchester, 1953).
[2] A recent translation by Count Potocki of Montalk (London, 1968) renders the title as *Forefathers*.

a political trial and a possessed man who challenges God. Słowacki's *Kordian* (1835) is a would-be assassin who fails to kill the Tsar. In both dramas the topicality of events and allusions increases the sense of violence. In both the monologue has an extended function and vibrates with stress and tension. The inner voice in it is a young voice asserting itself, no longer a well-measured tirade as in classical tragedy; now the words froth from the mouth, the possessed Konrad of Mickiewicz hurls them at God like some spittle of magic. By tradition this particular monologue is called the Great Improvisation and it reveals, most violently, the bardic heritage of the poet.[1] Earlier, at the age of twenty-two, he wrote an ode to Youth (*'Oda do młodości'*) which quickly outgrew its classical references and became a *Sturm und Drang* message, a robust incantation like that of Schiller's to Joy, *'An die Freude'*, or his welcome to the new century (*'Der Antritt des neuen Jahrhunderts'*). Appropriately, the 'Ode to Youth' was printed in Warsaw during the revolution.

Mickiewicz was to end as a poet of silence, baffling and, no doubt, himself baffled by his sudden withdrawal from literature. He wrote *Pan Tadeusz*, his last major work, twenty-one years before his death. But this is another story which will be discussed in a later chapter. What, however, remained from his early romanticism was a self-generated conviction in his bardic mission which others for patriotic reasons were only too eager to accept. Moreover, it gave the young Polish poets to come an authority to which they could refer their own claims. The younger they were, the more bardic and Messianic they felt.

As recently as 1956 when the Stalinist orthodoxy crashed in 'the spring of October', poets could find no better banners to display than the romantic ones. Some almost seemed to imply that their poetic incantations to freedom were responsible for the liberalization of politics. Would they be prepared to accept an equal measure of responsibility for the retreat from the ideals of October 1956? I wonder.

But the Stalinist years have left in Poland as well as in Hungary a serious dissatisfaction with the claims of poetry. Many young poets had, after all, corrupted their talent in the service of the totalitarian state. Their adolescent fervour was

[1] *Dziady*, Part III, Act I, Scene 2. During his stay in Russia Mickiewicz acquired fame for his improvisations in literary salons, as that of Princess Zinaida Volkonsky.

spent on one word of incantation: the tyrant's name. 'You have poured all your thought into the Party.' 'Your word marks out a new course for rivers.'[1] 'We shall call the future by His name.'[2] Such phrases in scores of volumes run into a long catalogue of epithets. But the catalogue itself cannot be explained away by a mistaken adoption of a wrong cause. Those who made it possible were clerks of literature, some juvenile and naïve, but all paid for providing the required panegyrics. Rimbaud would have used a crude word to describe their effort.

3

The weakness of adolescent incantations lies in their appeal to some vaguely ultimate reality while the realities of experience are considered inferior, merely filling up a prosaic pattern of events. Hence boredom, ennui, *taedium vitae* affecting poets who are not old enough to be tired of life but think the passage of days irrelevant to their vision. It matters little whether they give a political or a religious meaning to their ultimate reality. A vision attached to a revolution can be as contemptuous of facts as a spiritual paradise imagined away from earthly conditions. A magician is needed to make words seem tangible and immediate so that one might share his contempt for the routine of things.

In countries like Poland where literature had to serve also as a substitute for the loss of political independence, the poet magician was readily accepted and consequently encouraged with trust. Young writers had a better chance than older ones. They did not fear the burden of a mission because they wrote in advance of experience, the weight of words being quite bearable for them. This had the appearance of courage. It is

[1] Twoje życie nie jest 'prywatne',
życiorys Twój to 'Kurs WKP(b)',
Tyś myśl całą swą przelał w Partię,
chłopsko-robotniczy żar Komunisty,
i rzekom nowy bieg wyznacza słowo Twe.
From Andrzej Braun's '*Człowiek*' (1) in *Reportaż serdeczny* (Cordial Reportage) (Warsaw, 1951).

[2] Wrogów zmieciemy. Przyszłość
Nazwiemy Jego imieniem.
From Artur Międzyrzecki's '*Marzec 1953*' in *Noc noworoczna* (A New Year's Night) (Warsaw, 1953).

therefore not surprising that in the Romantic era Poles acquired the dangerous habit of looking to the young for guidance. Today this habit is by no means restricted to Poles.

The adolescent magic of incantation, however, has to end in a conflict when experience catches up with words, and the poet has to make good his claims, first of all, to himself. This is his test and his crisis. For he may not survive as a poet on reaching maturity.

CHAPTER II

FROM COUNTER-MAGIC TO SUICIDE

I

On the island of magic, Caliban is a slave to poetry and music. Both disarm his violent passions, lulling him to sleep with sounds that give delight and open rich clouds in his dreams. Caliban cannot partake of Prospero's power: his experience of magic must remain passive. The only counter-magic available to him is language. He tells his master Prospero:

> You taught me language; and my profit on't
> Is, I know how to curse: the red plague rid you,
> For learning me your language![1]

Dramatically, *The Tempest* works through the relationship between the elemental force which is Caliban, and the art which is Prospero; theirs is the unsteady state of the poetic cosmology. Those who cast spells and those who are spell-bound need one another to prove that there is superior power over the elements. Caliban has Prospero's language, and curses can therefore be his self-defence.

An eighteenth-century poet, Robert Lloyd, shows the muse in an urban habitation. No more island, full of bewitching noises. The distrust this time is rational, and the musical noise is made by the rhyme, almost casually:

> The harlot muse, so passing gay,
> Bewitches only to betray.[2]

The harlot becomes a destructive phantom for the romantic poet whenever he is in conflict with his muse. Count Henryk, the hero of Krasiński's drama *Nieboska komedia* (The Undivine Comedy, 1835), curses the phantom he has pursued to the

---

[1] *The Tempest*, Act I, Scene 2.
[2] From 'The Temple of Favour', in *The Poetical Works of Robert Lloyd* (London, 1774), vol. II.

destruction of himself and those who love him. The phantom cursed is poetry. Now this use of counter-magic by a possessed man has a double significance: it confirms the power of words in the very act of denying them their ultimate reality; it also shows the way in which the crisis of adolescence occurs.

Zygmunt Krasiński was himself very young when he wrote *The Undivine Comedy*, a drama far more impressive in its psychological and social concepts than in the execution, which suffers from rapid changes of scene and careless dialogue. Its main social concept was undoubtedly original for 1835. Presented as a vision of the future, it concerns the final phase of the class struggle in which the remaining defenders of the old aristocratic order are annihilated on the ramparts of Holy Trinity Castle.[1] Their leader, Count Henryk, commits suicide, his life of action ending in self-destruction, more conclusive in the physical sense than the death of poetry within him. The link between the two suicides has a special interest. The cursed phantom of poetry is transformed into the phantom of politics, to be exorcized this time not by the poet's own counter-magic, but by the apocalyptic sign of the cross in the sky after the ultimate battle of mankind.[2]

More significant still are the personal elements transformed in the play. Like his hero, Krasiński was an aristocrat and a poet. Dominated by the powerful personality of his father, from which he could not free himself even as an adult, Krasiński found in poetry the only source of strength, and though he published his works under pseudonyms or anonymously,[3] the bardic sense of mission possessed him throughout his restless and, for the most part, unhappy life. His literary contemporaries, Mickiewicz and Słowacki, responded to the visionary manifestations in his writing. However sceptical one is today about the romantic type of insight, one cannot fail to recognize in Krasiński a faculty at work which might be defined as a pro-

---

[1] Though intended to be symbolic, the place is authentic: Okopy Świętej Trójcy, in the south-east corner of Poland, close to the pre-1939 frontier with Soviet Russia.

[2] The leader of the victorious 'democrats' sees it before his death. This supernatural epilogue has been criticized as an unwarranted extension of the content, but to me it seems in keeping with the magical interventions throughout the play.

[3] The English study of Zygmunt Krasiński by Monica Gardner is appropriately entitled, *The Anonymous Poet of Poland* (Cambridge, 1919).

phetic gift. In *The Undivine Comedy*, for instance, the leader of the world revolution is described as bald with yellow skin and 'a high wide forehead', he has a black beard and 'staring eyes fixed on his listeners'—a curiously hypnotic pre-portrait of Lenin. There are many other puzzling examples of foresight, both social and religious, which can be found in Krasiński's works and letters: a vision of St. John's Church replacing that of St. Peter[1] comes as a double surprise from a man who was, if anything, a dogmatic Roman Catholic.

But in his private thoughts, too, disillusionment haunts him in shapes later to become recognizable. Ten years before his marriage, which was to be a loveless arrangement characteristic of his class, Krasiński depicted the marital relationship between Count Henryk and Maria with penetrating precision. The virginal apparition (*Dziewica*) symbolizing poetry has thus no difficulty in enticing the Count away from the marriage bed.

At this point the analogy with Shelley almost asserts itself. Both poets adhere to the essence of Romanticism in personal and aesthetic matters. They are at their best when using up their adolescent intelligence in the attempt to comprehend and embrace all: contemporary events as well as history and myth; they fall easily into the bathos of incantation when their bardic voice is pitched high (as in Shelley's 'Ode to Liberty' or 'Ode to Heaven', and Krasiński's 'Psalms of the Future'). In their private life both seemed unable to distinguish between the romantic sanctity of love and a messy entanglement of emotions. Krasiński's correspondence with Delfina Potocka, his mistress and muse, is revealing equally as the record of great intellectual powers and of persistently immature feelings. Shelley's naïvety in dealing with his wives and mistresses could almost have passed for angelic innocence, had it not been for the tragic consequences of his behaviour. Both he and Krasiński had the same cerebral precociousness[2] which seems to have arrested their adolescent growth and brought about a serious crisis. For this reason they were later open to criticism distrustful of their motives and often prejudiced.[3]

[1] In *Legenda*, 1840. The collapsing dome of St. Peter's literally buries the Pope.
[2] Krasiński had two novels published at the age of eighteen.
[3] After the last war, Krasiński was made into the scapegoat of Polish Romanticism by Communist pundits. Since 1960, however, the tone has changed in most essays about him (e.g. *Zygmunt Krasiński. W stulecie śmierci*, Warsaw, 1960).

But Krasiński the romantic accuser of poetry, as opposed to
Krasiński the histrionic bard, stands out against the confusion
of incantations: his adolescent genius in *The Undivine Comedy*
expresses, I think, with intuitive understanding, the psychic
dilemma of an early creative process.

2

The Undivine Comedy consists of four parts, each preceded by a
prologue written in rhythmic prose. These prologues are the
most sustained experiments in the manner of incantation, based
on Biblical cadences. They give the impression that the action,
to which the introductory incantations allude in turn, takes
place *sub specie aeternitatis*. In the prologue to Part One a clear
distinction is made between the poetry of either recollection or
premonition and the poetry of a living contemporaneity close to
experience, unmediated by imagination.

Krasiński is, in fact, saying something similar to Wordsworth's dictum about emotion recollected in tranquillity,[1] or to
Coleridge's probing into the nature of imagination.[2] Such ideas
were afloat in the Romantic air everywhere, in Germany,
England, and Poland. Krasiński, however, used the distinction
for a purpose which is his and his hero's concern: what exactly
is destructive in the poet's calling? Surely, not 'The Mother of
Beauty and Salvation', for these are the epithets applied to
poetry by Krasiński. But unfortunate is he who in the worlds
about to perish must recollect or intimate poetry. The next
statement leaves no doubt about the possessive character of
this necessity. Only those, Krasiński says, who have wholly
devoted themselves to poetry are destroyed by it; only those
who have become the living voices of its glory.[3]

If we consider this passage in the light of Count Henryk's
story, the meaning of possession has an intriguing dual facet.
The poet prophet speaks through the intimation of the past as
well as the future, for a voice possessed by poetry echoes recollec-

[1] Preface to *Lyrical Ballads*, 1798.
[2] *Biographia Literaria*, chapters 4, 13, 22.
[3] I quote the relevant passage in Polish: 'Ten tylko nieszczęśliwy, kto na
światach poczętych, na światach mających zginąć musi wspominać lub przeczuwać
ciebie—bo jedno tych gubisz, którzy się poświęcili tobie, którzy się stali żywymi
głosami twej chwały.'

tion in much the same way as it divines future happenings. Both functions come from a memory without chronology which is poetry's own memory. I am inclined to extend this interpretation further: the memory with no chronology could be considered as the true source of imagination.

Now Krasiński is consistent when showing the poetic psyche at work in the character of Count Henryk. His lack of faith in the aristocratic cause he has chosen to defend does not contradict his positive decision to follow the course of action after renouncing poetry. He cannot believe in the class which his intellect regards as doomed to perish, but since he is also a possessed man, his voice speaks for the glory of the feudal past in the celebrated scene in Part Three when he finally meets his opponent Pankracy, a visionary like himself and also a possessed genius. The world about to end together with its all-inclusive poetic memory, must allow the possessed voices to release that total memory. And in the closing scene after the battle on the Holy Trinity Ramparts the enemy of God, Pankracy, is made to acknowledge Christ's ultimate victory in the cry '*Galilaee vicisti*', which is both an echo from a remote past[1] and a fulfilment of prophecy.

There is a minor character in *The Undivine Comedy* who helps to elucidate the moral implications of the plot and mediates between the two stages in Count Henryk's story, his private and public life. He is Henryk's only son Orcio, a child poet who goes blind at fourteen.[2] The gift inherited from his father jars against this physical deprivation. Orcio's eyes, which can see far beyond reality, cannot see its immediate contours. Again the connexion between poetic possession and suffering is emphasized. For Orcio's possession is the result of his mother's will, who wanted him to be a poet so that through him she could transform her own love for Henryk into a living poetry.

In Part Four Orcio accompanies his father down into the vaults of Holy Trinity Castle: the battle is nearly over and the blind son, victim of poetry, has to mediate in transmitting the

---

[1] The cry is traditionally attributed to Emperor Julian the Apostate, who renounced Christianity.

[2] This blindness is a personal experience. Already in childhood Krasiński suffered from bad sight and had sporadic attacks of blindness. The blind visionary is of course a poetic archetype, personified by Homer and Milton, but here he is significantly a child.

voices which curse his father. The child poet hears and sees beyond darkness. From the chorus of voices comes this condemnation: 'Since you have loved nothing, admired nothing, except yourself and your thoughts, you are damned, damned for all eternity.'

In a later scene Count Henryk is cursed by a real person, his old and faithful servant, who commends him to the powers of hell. And it is then, the battle and all hope being lost, that Henryk utters his own magic, paying back the price of his possession with the curse of evil: 'Poetry be damned as I myself shall be damned for ever!'[1]

Counter-magic, however, requires the same sacrifice as magic received or inherited: Count Henryk knows this instinctively and offers his physical existence by throwing himself from the ramparts into a crevasse. The question remains open whether or not the curse delivered against poetry will free the poet's spirit from the memory of his possession. Probably not, if poetry is memory stronger than time, containing not only the present but the imagined before and after.

Krasiński was too involved, in the personal as well as the prophetic sense, to give an ultimate answer in *The Undivine Comedy*. He wrote it out of his own adolescent crisis; the condemnation of his visionary gift seems to be implied in the progress of Count Henryk in whom one senses the poet's self-hatred and also his profound understanding of the poetic possession. Other Romantic writers sought escape in death-dreams or in the mystical disavowal of sensual beauty; some abandoned writing altogether; a few elected by fate found an early death.

Krasiński lived until he was forty-seven. 'Within these lungs I have carried a heavy coffin, my own heart,' he said in a lyrical poem[2] and translated St. Teresa's gloss about death (*'que muero porque no muero'*) with a personal feeling for its paradoxes. As he grew older he came to accept the dissatisfaction with poetry which originated in the great crisis of his adolescence, and which brought a sense of artistic limitation. He even wrote a short lyric confessing his inability to write a perfect poem, and this confession is particularly meaningful. I quote it entire in an English rendering:

[1] In the original: *'Poezjo, bądź mi przeklęta, jako ja sam będę na wieki!'*
[2] *'Znad wód'* (Over the waters).

God has denied me the angelic measure
That marks a poet in the world of thought.
Had I possessed it earth would become a treasure
But I'm a rhymer since I have it not.

Oh, my heart rings with heavenly zones of sound
But ere they reach my lips they break apart.
Men hear a clattering when I'm around
But day and night I hear my aching heart.

It beats against my waves of blood: a star
Rings in the vast blue whirlpool of the sky.
Men in their festive halls don't hear so far:
God listens to the star until it dies.[1]

3

The ideal poetry then is the one which communicates directly
and therefore has no need of possession. But this at once raises
the most difficult problem of all. Is any language of poetry a
possessed language? If so, the poet free of possession could be
imagined creating outside—or rather, without—language, in
some unrecordable form moulded from silence. The aim of this
study is to explore the conditions which bring the writer to that
other side of poetry. They have to be considered in both psychological and aesthetic terms before any definition of the state of
poetic silence can be attempted. In any case, one will be obliged
to use words in order to describe the absence of words. The task
is unavoidably difficult.

When Rimbaud cries out 'No more words', '*Plus de mots*',[2] he
is expressing a deep dissatisfaction with his medium, a medium
he has treated as magic. His predecessor Baudelaire felt much
the same in the *Spleen* poems, and before him some of the great
possessed among the Romantics. On occasions even a minor
talent fondly attached to words would realize that the attachment was in itself a trap. Conrad's father, Apollo Korzeniowski,
wrote these opening lines to a rather indifferent poem:

---

[1] Jerzy Peterkiewicz and Burns Singer, *Five Centuries of Polish Poetry* (London,
1960).
[2] *Mauvais sang.*

Thoughts tangle up and words grow numb.
Eyelids drop like coffin lids. . . .[1]

The temptation to opt out altogether and be neither a possessed victim nor a trumpeter of hollow incantations led a number of poets to suicide, but the suicides finally committed usually had their neurotic beginning in late adolescence. They were rooted in unresolved conflicts, and each conflict went by way of negation: first poetry was cursed as an apparition, an abstraction, and when this did not work, the medium had to be personified, so that it could be challenged more effectively, and in the process of transference the personification became a person, the poet himself, who was now at least able to put poetry to death.

Goethe's Werther would not have passed so quickly from a sentimental novel of debatable merit to a literary model and then a myth, had not the crisis latent in all adolescence demanded this formulation of itself in a human individual who wore a yellow waistcoat and could express his sensibility without offending elegance. Werther writes in his diary on 22 August 1771: '. . . my active powers are dulled into a restless lassitude, and I cannot do anything, either. I have no power of imagination, no feeling for nature, and books disgust me.'[2]

This goes beyond the self-analysis of eighteenth-century women in epistolary fiction. Yet the tone of Werther's introspection must have attracted the feminine element in adolescence, on whose creative stimuli artists depended and were naturally anxious to retain when becoming mature.

For the young Słowacki, who was brought up among women,[3] the feminine psyche was a driving force in writing and in friendship. Suicide, however, disturbed it early—not a Wertherian influence, but a fact: his former school friend, a brilliant

---

[1] 'Myśli się plączą i słowa niemieją./Powieka spada, jako wieko trumny. . . .' '*Myśli się plączą*' in the volume *Komedia i Strofy oderwane* (Wilno, 1856), published a year before Joseph Conrad's birth.

[2] *The Sufferings of Young Werther*, translated by Bayard Quincy Morgan (London, 1957), Book I.

[3] Juliusz Słowacki, born 1809, was three years older than Krasiński. His mother married again and he spent his early years in the company of her two step-daughters. When he chose to live in exile after 1831, his attachment to his mother remained and is beautifully recorded in his letters to her, which are the chief source of his biography. I shall quote from Słowacki's mystical notes in Chapter IX.

Orientalist, shot himself in 1827 in a manor house in Polish Lithuania. For the nineteen-year-old poet this was a traumatic experience, from which he tried to absolve his memory in *Godzina myśli* (The Hour of Thought, 1832), a long and well-sustained reflective poem. It could be argued that the shock of the experience and his analysis of it in *The Hour of Thought* helped Słowacki to mature as artist and man. For this reason perhaps there is later a remarkable lack of aberration in his Messianic pronouncements on the state of exile politics, even in his most ardent utterances during a brief period of involvement with the religious fanatic Towiański. What makes *The Hour of Thought* an important work is its honest and authoritative treatment of the adolescent crisis resulting from the romantic infatuation with suicide on the one hand, i.e. with immature death in Rilke's sense of ripening death, and with instant mysticism on the other. The poem describes how the two young men fed their imagination on a memory, intuitive and ancient, not their own.

> In their day-dreaming they understood the cryptic books
> Which their thoughts couldn't grasp. From childish sand
> They built castles on Swedenborg's tracts
> Full of angelic voices, madness and light.

The dangerous game with innate knowledge and presentiments ended for one of them in a violent escape from reality, and that single pistol shot startled the poet into accepting life. Despite a very unsuccessful courtship of fame, his body gradually weakened by tuberculosis, Słowacki grew inwardly stronger and reached a state when he could accept death with simplicity.

In discussing the literary causes of suicide one has, for the sake of clarity, to keep them separate from medical implications, however true these may be in another context. Among Goethe's friends in the *Sturm und Drang* period, the restless Merck killed himself in 1791;[1] the English jester of death, Beddoes, who loved Germany, poisoned himself in 1849, leaving a note pinned on his body ('. . . I ought to have been, among a variety of other things, a good poet'). The romantic Wertheromania is probably less mysterious to a psychiatrist. Of 'the experience of negation' R. D. Laing writes:

[1] Wilhelm Jerusalem's suicide in 1772 had already made the concept of Werther both credible and shocking.

c

The silence of the preformation expressed in and through language, cannot be expressed by language. . . . A man may indeed produce something new—a poem, a pattern, a sculpture, a system of ideas—think thoughts never before thought, produce sights never before seen. Little benefit is he likely to derive from his own creativity. The phantasy is not modified by such 'acting out', even the sublimest. The fate that awaits the creator, after being ignored, neglected, despised, is, luckily or unluckily according to point of view, to be discovered by the non-creative. There are sudden, apparently inexplicable suicides that must be understood as the dawn of a hope so horrible and harrowing that it is unendurable.[1]

Similarly, a serious analyst of politics could offer a straightforward explanation of Mayakovsky's suicide. When he shot himself in 1930, less than thirteen years after the Bolshevik revolution, the officials of Soviet literature with their customary hypocrisy first frowned on this individualistic departure from the earthly paradise, then put the propagandist on a higher monument, restored his tough image and covered up his final despair. In 1935 Stalin pronounced Mayakovsky the best poet of the Soviet era.

The biographical facts concerning Mayakovsky's suicide may have the appearance of obscurity, but their meaning in relation to his poetry, his temperament, and his revolutionary faith are not difficult to understand. Besides, even censored history yields a few documents to truth after some delay.

Mayakovsky condemned himself to death as soon as he became one of the accusers of poetry. His anger could not stop at words. Nor could it stop at silence, for this would be outside the reach of any political censorship. In a poem addressed to Sergey Esenin who took his own life in a shabby Leningrad hotel at the end of December 1925, Mayakovsky had to protest against such an exit, 'It's not hard to die in our life',[2] yet the example of the poet he respected became a pointer to his own self-destruction, five years later. In his grotesque plays (such as *The Bedbug*, 1929) he was at least able to muffle his anger by rapidly changing his scenes and his mood. But lyrical incantation does not allow for such evasive measures. I quote from an

---

[1] *The Politics of Experience and The Bird of Paradise* (London, 1967), chapter I, 6.

[2] '*Sergeyu Eseninu*' (To Sergey Esenin).

unfinished poem which was found in Mayakovsky's pocket at
the time of his death.

> ... Why bother then
> To balance mutual sorrows, pains and hurts.
> Behold what quiet settles on the world.
> Night wraps the sky in tribute from the stars.[1]

If this was intended to be the last poem, then it expresses the
curious calm of a man poised on a ledge, ready to plunge down
and also ready to jump back. At such a time, he says at the very
end of the fragment, 'one rises to address the ages, history, and
all creation', but the address did not come. Instead, a bullet
closed this act of creation.

The suicidal character of Esenin has had many apologists,
partly because his lyrical verse is one continuous apologia for
the village paradise imprudently abandoned, and for his own
loss of innocence resulting, it seems, from poetic commitment
alone.

> ... For ever
> I've forsaken my friends and my home.
> The poplars will sound no longer
> Their fluttering leaves over my head.
> My hovel will fall down without me,
> And my dog has croaked long ago.
> God has condemned me to die
> On the tortuous streets of Moscow.[2]

He is a poet who wants nothing to alter his state of being
suspended in a spiritual fall. His suicide was not even contem-
plated, it happened to him once he set out from his native
village Konstantinovo. The people he met during his urban
sleep-walking felt that they could give him no help. Even their
sympathy had an air of being presumptuous. A person as ego-
centric as Isadora Duncan sensed the total separateness of
Esenin when they travelled together during their brief marriage,
he out of place everywere, in Europe and in America, and
drunk most of the time. A poet and a dancer, the two were only
suited to some abstract idea of an artistic couple; everything
else remained incongruous and had to end in failure. His

---

[1] '*Uzhe vtoroi*' (Past one o'clock), translated by George Reavey, in *Modern
European Poetry*, op. cit.

[2] '*Moskva Kabatskaya*' (Tavern Moscow), translated by George Reavey, op. cit.

Russia of birches and ploughed fields seemed static from a distance, but it was an illusion of memory, and memory alone could not heal his 'restless misery'.[1]

Esenin's death, though self-inflicted, had about it the same inevitability as the death of Dylan Thomas in New York, to which, judging from the printed accounts by his wife and an American friend, he drove himself through a drunken stupor. Again an adolescent myth surrounds his departure from life and poetry. His voice has remained alive on gramophone records, still imprisoned by the magic from which he wanted to escape. Perhaps the release is never complete for those who, like Caliban, 'know how to curse'.

A curious anthology appeared in 1963, containing eighty-four poems, all of them paying tribute to Dylan Thomas.[2] It is a revealing document. Keats, the romantic Adonis, had Shelley the eternal adolescent to glorify his name; a modern Adonis has a whole chorus of elegies to his credit. None of them compares with the quality of *Adonais*. But they all have this in common with Shelley: there is a tone of envy in the homages to the death of a young man—yes, he timed his exit well, he did not allow himself to look older than his verse. He managed to conjure up his death, so he was a magician after all.

Those who now react strongly against the Dylan Thomas myth are perhaps defending literature as a discipline, believing that it should master a creative growth, however wild and destructive. But they may also be expressing another kind of envy: that fame should be so identical with myth as to invalidate any critical objection from the accusers. 'Your life and death remind us of ourselves.'[3] An honest line, certainly. For it can be read both ways, as praising and accusing, an apologia for no-more-apology.

---

[1] From '*Pismo k materi*' (Letter to my mother). In post-war Poland an analogous suicide occurred. Stanisław Piętak, born 1909, a gifted poet of peasant origin, could not adjust his authentic village themes to the essentially urban mode of contemporary literature. He killed himself in 1964. His last book of verse is *Zaklinania* (Spells, 1963), a title most significant in its appeal to counter-magic. See chapter V.

[2] *A Garland for Dylan Thomas*, compiled by George J. Firmage (New York, 1963). The selection of poems was made 'from almost 150 written in tribute to Thomas over the past ten years'.

[3] Robert Pack, 'On the Death of Dylan Thomas', from *A Garland for Dylan Thomas*.

4

I have not dealt with those adolescents who get out of poetry the easiest way, without cursing it and without committing suicide, physical or spiritual. There seems to be a negligible dust of regret deposited on those slim volumes of verse as the years go by and their authors establish themselves, each in his new and more practical profession. In the end they are bemused by the recollection that they once thought themselves inspired. Why should there be this single flowering of inspiration, however unenduring its results in the pages of a solitary volume?

The Freudian interpreters of the creative process tend to ascribe this brief spell of youthful self-expression to sexual urges. Writing is regarded as a compensation for unfulfilled desires. In his autobiography the novelist Rayner Heppenstall tells us, with an ironic wink, at what age exactly the adolescent habits change, making the scribbling of verse superfluous: 'The age of twenty-five may also be that at which most people as they adopt a regular sexual habit, abandon that auto-eroticism of the imagination which may be thought quite normal in civilised youth.'[1]

Marinetti was thirty-three when he published his 'Manifesto of Futurism'. Seven years more for him, and then: 'When we are forty let younger and stronger men than we throw us in the waste paper basket like useless manuscripts!'[2]

Military action apart, Marinetti glorified the war of generations, and this flattered the young for a time. Some people still take an extreme view and consider all poetry to be a youthful activity. Wordsworth and Tennyson, they feel, wrote nothing truly original in their old age. They prefer early Goethe and early Pound.[3] But this opinion could be refuted with the ex-

---

[1] *The Intellectual Part* (London, 1963), p. 64.

[2] The Manifesto appeared in *Le Figaro* on 20 February 1909.

[3] At twenty-eight Pound wrote:

It is true that most people poetize more or less, between the ages of seventeen and twenty-three. The emotions are new, and, to their possessor, interesting, and there is not much mind or personality to be moved. As the man, as his mind, becomes a heavier and heavier machine, a constantly more complicated structure, it requires a constantly greater voltage of emotional energy to set it in harmonious motion. It is certain that the emotions increase in vigour as a vigorous man matures. . . . Most important poetry has been written by men over thirty.

'The Serious Artist', from *The Egoist*, 1913, reprinted in *Literary Essays of Ezra Pound* (London, 1954).

ample of Victor Hugo, improving as a poet at the end of his life.
Yeats wrote extraordinary verse in his seventies, and did not
think this odd. A sexo-centric expert, however, would immedi-
ately add something about Hugo's exceptional virility and
about Yeats undergoing the Steinach operation in his sixty-
ninth year. Yeats himself answered his inquisitive critics in the
lines:

> You think it horrible that lust and rage
> Should dance attention upon my old age;
> They were not such a plague when I was young;
> What else have I to spur me into song?[1]

Yet this sort of defence, if taken as a rational argument, turns
the problem of age round again and brings adolescence back to
its previous prominence. Whether we like it or not, we have to
concede that the primeval forces of poetry, inspiration and
magic, both sanctified by popular tradition, suit the youthful
image of the poet. The wise old man, courting his lady muse
with lyrical songs, looks somewhat ridiculous as most old men
in love do. Robert Graves may see in the divine lady the source
of inspiration, timeless and unpredictably generous,[2] but like
most of her priestesses on earth she frequently shows a marked
preference for the adolescent who blackmails her with suicide
rather than for the respectful bard aged in the service of poetry.

Only occasionally a poet obsessed with death knows in spite
of his young years that no solution is easy, no exit from life
assured of eternal comforts.

> That death might not be casual,
> Flick thumbing ash in the swish of a squint draught,
> Lint pad for a bruise-eyed nation.
> Bandage to blindfold memories that laughed;
> That death might not be an empty flesh-felt gesture:
>
> That hereafter might not be fed
> With mutes mad and the sane ones poor and scared,
> An asylum from single beds,

---

[1] 'The Spur', from *Last Poems*, 1936–1939. See also 'The Wild Old Wicked Man'
in the same volume.

[2] *The White Goddess* (London, 1948). Even more revealing is his talk about this
book, delivered in New York on 9 February 1957, and published in the volume *Steps*
(London, 1958). Graves attributes the sinister deaths of two publishers who rejected
The White Goddess to the regal displeasure of the Lunar Muse.

From the profane ignorance everywhere shared;
That God might not be a charitable institution for the dead.[1]

The accusing voice here reaches out, beyond the medium of language and its magical façade. To me at least it seems to be travelling now towards the other side of silence.

[1] Burns Singer, 'Epilogue' from *Still and All* (London, 1957). Burns Singer died suddenly of a heart attack in 1964, aged thirty-seven.

CHAPTER III

THE MATURE ACTIVISTS

I

It would be naïve to suggest that the survival of the poet in maturity is necessarily the survival of the fittest artist. The second-raters have, on the whole, a better chance of adjusting their talent to new conditions of work which require less incantation and more skill in the craft of verse. They are not easily tempted either by the demands of the muse or the demands of ideals. Their reward is an election to some academy of letters, a literary prize on the occasion of a jubilee, twenty-five or fifty years of being a practitioner of verse.

There is, however, another and more interesting progress of a mature poet. The temptations he has to face lead him away from the practice of his art, and the strongest of them is service to a grand cause. By then the poet possesses sufficient experience and also sufficient caution not to use his pen unduly, his distrust of all rhetorical statements being based on his timely rejection of incantation. Yet his own reputation gives him at the same time a confident excuse for not writing. He is now on active service. Should some begin to regard him as a dead poet, he would not be offended. A poet killed in action, even metaphorically speaking, sounds plausibly acceptable.

For the nineteenth century, Byron was the poet of action, a man who exchanged a romantic traveller's cloak for a soldier's dress. It did not matter that he had not died while fighting; the fever that killed him at Missolonghi would have created a heroic myth out of the Greek place-name alone. What counted was Byron's honourable intention. Outside England, many of his admirers knew little about the circumstances of his death. To them his was a hero's end. Byron's gesture in no way resembled that of a poet-journalist reporting from behind the front lines, as some of the propagandists of the cause did during the Spanish civil war. The nearest analogy in this century was Rupert Brooke's death on the way to the Dardanelles: his burial on Scyros, the island of Achilles, sealed his war sonnets with an aura of myth.

Byron wrote his last significant poem at Missolonghi on 22 January 1824, his thirty-sixth birthday,[1] and it offers a psychological key to his life of action. In a tone of unmistakable sincerity he questions the validity of his passions. Each stanza in turn speaks of the emotional exhaustion which, however, does not appear to be the usual romantic languor. On the contrary, it strikes one as an attempt to describe accurately the successive states of mind when the choice has suddenly been understood:

> Awake! (not Greece—she *is* awake!)
> Awake, my spirit! Think through *whom*
> Thy life-blood tracks its parent lake,
> And then strike home!
>
> Tread those reviving passions down,
> Unworthy manhood!—unto thee
> Indifferent should the smile or frown
> Of beauty be.
>
> If thou regret'st thy youth, *why live?*
> The land of honourable death
> Is here:—up to the field, and give
> Away thy breath![2]

The death wish has reached the surface, but this time it is 'the land of honourable death' where the sense of history means also a very personal sense of duty. Byron's Greece therefore is more than a cause, just as his duty goes beyond choosing. He knows there is nothing equally precise to define his absent passions. 'The worm, the canker and the grief are mine alone.' No rhetoric in this statement at the end of the second stanza. In the sixth ('glory and Greece') and in the seventh ('Awake, my spirit!') Byron falls back on the technique of incantation; it is a half-hearted leap towards ecstasy, unconvincing in each exclamation mark. Real action needs no words to spur itself, it has

---

[1] 'On this day I complete my thirty-sixth year', published posthumously in *The Morning Chronicle*, 29 October 1824, as 'Lord Byron's Latest Verses'.

[2] Compare this final seriousness with the lines from *Don Juan*, Canto VII, 4:
> For my part, I pretend not to be Cato,
> Not even Diogenes—We live and die,
> But which is best, you know no more than I.

to exist, it has to become a recordable fact, and Byron knows this well.[1]

Since action means stepping beyond poetry, if only for a moment of risk, it takes Byron away from the rhetoric of death and brings him close to the honourable reality of his own death. 'A soldier's grave' which he seeks can therefore be regarded as an obvious consequence of his action and also as a verdict condemning poetry *in absentia*. 'Choose thy ground' is still a rhetorical command at the end of a poem; the real choice came much earlier in the double sense of history and duty, the first not realizable without the other.

Yet it was the poetry of Byron which the Greek episode ultimately protected against hostile criticism and biographical bias. No matter how often the critics attributed insincerity to Byron's writing, his death at Missolonghi exempted some verses at least from a derogatory charge. He saved his poetic face for those who can never separate biography from literature. Once this exemption was admitted, Byron the poet remained to be sought in his other works as well. Today his *Vision of Judgement* and *Beppo* are singled out for praise, and the virtuosity of *Don Juan*, which has always been duly noted, is credited to poetic invention apart from metrical skill.

For the Spaniard José de Espronceda (1808–1842), who modelled himself on Byron, action was as spontaneous as inspiration.[2] He fought on the barricades of Paris in the July revolution of 1830 and wanted to go to Poland where an insurrection broke out a few months later. Always prepared to test his republican ideas in practice, Espronceda took risks; *El diablo mundo*, his Faustian poem, has the strength and weakness resulting from the same casual approach to the business of writing as characterizes the best and the worst of Byron. For Espronceda living was a poetic commitment; the craftsman's trials were unimportant to him.

---

[1] Byron despised his own literary *genus*: 'I do think the preference of *writers* to *agents*—the mighty stir made about scribbling and scribes, by themselves and others—a sign of effeminacy, degeneracy and weakness. Who would write, who had anything better to do?' (*Journal*, 24 November 1813).

[2] The rebel myth of Byron suited also the revolutionary aspirations of the South American continent, in which writers were involved. Juan Montalvo, a passionate admirer of Byron from Ecuador, opposed the dictator Garcia Moreno and, like the Argentinian poet Echeverría, died in exile.

One is tempted to speculate whether there exists, after all, such a phenomenon as the poetry of action which throws back on to the poetry of words a glow so edifying that the earlier words, unrelated to the action, seem to reflect it all the same, and thus gain in authority.[1] How protective is, in fact, the poet's instinct for choosing memorable action when his words are endangered and may be ignored by posterity?

If Byron sensed the need of a heroic myth for himself, he must also have understood the vulnerability of his art.

2

Adam Mickiewicz's decision to become a man of action resembled that of Byron. Its outcome, too, was similarly unexpected. Mickiewicz died in 1855 in Constantinople of cholera, not from a Russian bullet. A Polish legion was formed during the Crimean war and Mickiewicz went to Turkey to help in its organization and to prove himself in direct patriotic action.[2] A man of fifty-seven, prematurely aged, he could at that time have been described without malice as a dead poet: he had written virtually nothing for twenty years. During that period he was a teacher, first in the Swiss academy at Lausanne, then in the Collège de France; he was also editor of a weekly in French (*La Tribune des Peuples*), and finally a librarian in a post which was a humble sinecure. Although his decision to go to Turkey resulted from his political activities, those who sponsored his mission (such as Prince Czartoryski, Zamoyski) still regarded him as a national bard, in some ways perhaps impractical, but in others most useful to Polish propaganda. His name counted.

Mickiewicz would have been a small asset to the cause with-

[1] This, for example, is how the Polish poet Norwid described the total effect of Byron's achievement: 'Byron is the Socrates of poets, because he was able to bring the poetic element into life and action with the full knowledge of what he was doing; and he supported this with thought, song, the energy of his activity . . . and finally with death. *Ecce poeta!*' (From the first lecture on Słowacki, *O Juliuszu Słowackim*, 1861.)

See also G. Wilson Knight, *Lord Byron: Christian Virtues* (London, 1952), chapter IV, 'Poetic Action'.

[2] His decision was no doubt prompted by the feeling of guilt that resulted from his hesitant behaviour after the outbreak of the November revolution in 1830. He intended then to join the insurgents, went to the Poznan district in Prussian Poland, but never crossed the frontier.

out his poetic achievement in the past. This was his spiritual passport to the life of action, and again like Byron, whom he admired and translated,[1] he felt the necessity of fitting his imaginary world to the dimension of practical action. His organizing abilities, as far as one can judge from documents, were not equal to Byron's. Nor was his personal magnetism capable of Byron's successes in leadership. He had, however, some experience of back-room politics during the revolutionary turmoil of 1848. He led a Polish legion in Italy on whose behalf he agitated quite effectively, but the legion itself was, numerically speaking, a paltry affair. In fact, even the reminiscences of sympathetic witnesses could not hide the disappointment at the sight of the marching legionaries. A certain G. A. Cesano recorded how on the first of May, 1848, a crowd gathered at the Porta Romana in Milan to greet the Polish soldiers. Instead of a legion, they saw an elderly figure followed by only eleven men, one of them a hunchback.[2] Mickiewicz, of course, was the pathetic figure marching at the head. If this illustrated the poet's defiance of the realities which other people could measure with their eyes, the defiance had not enough strength to romanticize the memories later when they came to be recorded.

How well did Mickiewicz remember the ironic lesson of 1848? Was he defying himself when he decided to go to Turkey?

Much more important for assessing Mickiewicz's motives seems to be the theme of dynamic action recurring in his works,[3] which always places his central characters in some moral predicament, whether it be a patriotic revenge through betrayal, as in *Konrad Wallenrod*, or a religious vow hiding a patriotic guilt, as in *Pan Tadeusz*. The character has to undergo a complete transformation, beginning with the adoption of a new name and new apparel.[4] But in each case the transformation cannot be achieved without some direct participation in action. An evil deed, though expiated in sacrifice, must be finally weighed again in the scales of action. Jacek Soplica in *Pan*

---

[1] He translated *The Giaour* (1835), a remarkable rendering in style.

[2] Cesano's *Ricordi* are mentioned by Stefan Kieniewicz in his book on Mickiewicz's Legion, *Legion Mickiewicza, 1848–1849* (Warsaw, 1957).

[3] For the apotheosis of life-force see the poem '*Farys*' (1829), in which the Bedouin's ride through the desert is described with great gusto.

[4] W. Borowy has lucidly examined this problem in his essay 'Poet of Transformation' (*Adam Mickiewicz*, edited by M. Kridl, New York, 1951).

Tadeusz, for instance, wears a monk's habit and leads the life of poverty, but he ends, as he began, by facing the dangers of battle.

And when the author's *alter ego* happens to be clearly personified, as in the drama *Dziady* (The Ancestors), the character is, in fact, a poet, again called Konrad. He tests his power of words in the supernatural sphere by challenging God, while in the world of action he is a prisoner awaiting deportation. The inactivity imposed here on the man of action surely has a symbolic meaning.

It is a matter for speculation whether Mickiewicz would have kept Konrad's poetic *persona* to the end of his drama. Would he have made the final redemptive action completely detached from poetry, that is from the illusory power of words? One fact points to this: the drama is an unfinished work, and not because it was meant to be so, in the romantic fashion of leaving masterpieces as monumental ruins. Mickiewicz intended *The Ancestors* to be his chief work, a Faustian expression of his life; he rated it above everything else he wrote. Even during his barren years after *Pan Tadeusz* he would return to *The Ancestors* and add scenes which he later destroyed. The drama was obviously conceived as an integrated whole despite the seeming whimsicality of the numbers which link the parts and fragments.[1] He wanted to complete this work because it was so unified as a spiritual concept, and it must have been a source of despair to see it abandoned by his imagination.

The significant fact remains that he did leave *The Ancestors* unfinished, and to whatever reason one ascribes this failure, it does not alter its relevance to the choice of action which, unconsciously perhaps, was the choice of death for the poet already dead. One of his late lyrics, written in Lausanne, begins with the line 'When my corpse takes a seat here in your midst' (*Gdy tu mój trup w pośrodku was zasiada*). It is not a macabre opening to a romantic ballad, but a personal statement.

Coleridge had enough intellectual courage to confess in a letter to Godwin (25 March 1801): 'The Poet is dead in me.' The capital 'p' looms there like an obelisk over a grave which is

---

[1] It has been suggested that Mickiewicz imitated Sterne in this respect, cf. W. Borowy, '*Zagadkowość w kompozycji* Dziadów *i próba jej wyjaśnienia*' (in *Studia i rozprawy*, Wrocław, 1952, vol. I).

still open. It was to remain open for thirty-three years until his physical death in 1834. The same honesty finally brought out a confession about his drug-addiction. 'I have in this one dirty business of Laudanum an hundred times deceived, tricked, nay, actually and consciously *lied*.' These words from a letter to John J. Morgan (14 May 1814) become even more poignant when one remembers that it is a dead poet exposing the terrible weakness of his body. And yet Coleridge wanted to fill the emptiness with action, and his action had to be systematized, regulated by some metaphysical order in the attempt to contain as much of life as possible. 'My system,' he said, 'is the only attempt I know ever made to reduce all knowledges into harmony.'[1] It was this harmonious system which he hoped to elaborate and hand down to posterity. But the great metaphysical book was never written.

Modern scholarship has revealed how original Coleridge was in his social and religious ideas,[2] but this had nothing to do with any direct participation. Coleridge was not a reformer; his lectures were the nearest thing to public action, yet still remained an expression of thought. Carlyle meant something essentially different when he said that 'the end of man is an action, and not a thought'.[3] Mickiewicz would have agreed with that, not Coleridge.

Earlier in his life, however, Coleridge knew he could give 'his eyes a magnifying power' and with them see 'phantoms of sublimity'.[4] At the end, accepting the failure of action, he summarized his last wishes in the epitaph for his own tomb. For many a year he had only 'found Death in Life'; as a Christian he could now legitimately hope to 'find Life in Death'.

Byron at least found 'the land of honourable death', and his poetry, though restless and often aimless, had in a sense guided him there. In Mickiewicz, as in Coleridge, the poet was dead already in the maturity which one of his last lyrics very aptly calls 'the age of defeat'.[5] All three poets recognized this, Byron earlier than Mickiewicz, and perhaps all felt in the end cheated by the choice of action.

[1] *Table Talk*, 12 September 1831.
[2] J. Colmer, *Coleridge: Critic of Society* (Oxford, 1959).
[3] *Sartor Resartus*, Book II, chapter 6.
[4] *Apologia pro vita sua.*
[5] '*Polały się łzy.*' The poem consists of only five lines.

3

In modern times, Yeats fully realized that there were limitations imposed by bardic poetry on action, and vice versa. His commitment to Irish nationalism in culture and in politics was undivided. He fought to establish the Irish theatre and succeeded; he admired the political activists John O'Leary and Maude Gonne, and identified himself with the rebels of Easter 1916. If a dreamy bard has to be responsible as well, *Responsibilities* (1914) is for Yeats a significant title. But the crisis he experienced in maturity was the crisis of poetic style. He lived, however, long enough to find himself disillusioned with his previous disillusionment. For, after all, history had caught up with his dreams. Soon after his exasperated cry, 'I am worn out with dreams',[1] Ireland became a free state in 1922 and in the same year he became one of its senators.

'When I got back here,' he wrote to Robert Bridges in January 1923, 'I found myself a senator and the Senate, though it does not break in upon my morning hours when I write verse etc., took away a large part of those afternoon hours when I write letters.' Occasionally he spoke at the sittings of the Senate. In 1926 he agreed to act as chairman of a committee which was to advise on a new coinage for the Irish state. He discharged his public duties, whatever they were worth. Action ceased to be an alternative to writing: it could hardly tempt when deflated to the level of everyday business. It was then that the craft demanded a revised account from its old practitioner. Whether Yeats cheated age or poetry by the rejuvenating operation in his sixty-ninth year seems to me immaterial. He became aware again of the artist's dilemma which he had already expressed in 1910;

> All things can tempt me from this craft of verse:
> One time it was a woman's face, or worse—
> The seeming needs of my fool-driven land;
> Now nothing but comes readier to the hand
> Than this accustomed toil.[2]

If the direct participation in the business of life can be outweighed, both as a need and as a duty, by the poet's accustomed

---

[1] From *The Wild Swans at Coole* (1917).
[2] From *The Green Helmet and other Poems* (1910).

toil, then the temptation of some active mission is reduced to a seeming duty, and the urgency of it disappears.

In this light one should, I think, better understand the crisis of commitment during the post-war period. Poet after poet suddenly saw the true mechanism of ideologies, most of them fool-driven and therefore collapsible. And if once he had acted as a naïve believer, an intimidated convert, or a bought propagandist, the action itself gave him a feeling of nausea. All over Eastern Europe after Stalin's death those who had been the activists of literature vomited their disgust with words into more words. And the craft of verse, even when devoid of inspiration, seemed now worth a renewed respect. There was no longer a threat of some high and distant alternative: a set of tools lay ready to hand.

4

It may appear from the argument in the previous pages that the mature poet is bound to be dissatisfied with action whenever he uses it as a potential cure against poetry. But this does not invalidate the experience obtained in the process, even though it may have been pursued merely to prove the unreality of poetry. The experience is an indubitable gain. Whether it can also immunize the poet is less certain.

For instead of being a potential cure, it may germinate a late poetic fever. Yeats the disillusioned man of action stands next to a new Yeats, the poet of lust and rage, speaking with the voice of Crazy Jane. I am not questioning this kind of experience. Nor am I attempting to disqualify the poet-activist for his lack of consistency. What I want to emphasize is the experience itself which, however regenerating it may be, does not reveal the other side of poetry. It ignores the necessity of silence as the incantations of adolescence ignored the necessity of experience.

How can we recognize the poet who is about to take the invisible road towards the horizon of silence? Socially, he seems a well-adjusted man, he has reached a secure age, he has had success. Nevertheless, he will contradict both his artistic and his social achievement by directing himself to the other side. The sign that marks him out clearly is his dissatisfaction with experience.

CHAPTER IV

LANGUAGE AS EXPERIENCE

I

At the age of fifty-two T. S. Eliot had the authority of experience behind him to be sceptical about experience and the wisdom associated with age. In the second section of *East Coker* he says:

> ... There is, it seems to us,
> At best, only a limited value
> In the knowledge derived from experience.

The tone is right, the qualifying phrases 'it seems to us' and 'at best' give a hesitant pause, suggesting perhaps that any comment on the nature of experience should be tentative. The lines that follow have a different assurance altogether:

> The knowledge imposes a pattern, and falsifies,
> For the pattern is new in every moment
> And every moment is a new and shocking
> Valuation of all we have been.

This continuous valuation is something we can test ourselves, whenever we allow any moment of our existence to stand out. Usually it passes on and is pulped into experience. The pattern within the moment can at any time invalidate that other pattern, imposed by knowledge, which has been extracted from the pulp of events. Eliot is, in fact, removing here the superiority attached to the so-called mature experiences, if by 'mature' we imply trusting the fixed patterns of knowledge. Dante's *nel mezzo del cammin* must therefore mean 'not only in the middle of the way but all the way, in a dark wood', and Eliot adds two analogous images, a bramble and a grimpen, where there is 'no secure foothold', because there cannot be security in the continuous action.

If we understand the full implication correctly, the poet has everything to gain by recognizing new patterns in new moments. His existence is in this sense always momentary. Once he lets himself become a slave to the seeming wisdom of experience,

D

he stops discovering real experience. Disillusionment with poetry may sometimes be no more than the dissatisfaction with experience, or rather with the trust put into it at the age of discretion. Neither the adolescent nor the mature poet has any certainty that he will get out quickly from the Dantesque wood.

I have dwelt on the distinctions made by Eliot in *East Coker*, because the poem itself is an illustration of the process through which the patterns of experience are shed in order to clarify at least a pattern of language. In this case the language has to establish a new pattern so that it may express negative states, one of them being the denial sequence from St. John of the Cross. Experience is thus equated with language, and here we have the essential paradox of the whole poem: the equation itself has no permanent value either.

> Because one has only learnt to get the better of words
> For the thing one no longer has to say, or the way in which
> One is no longer disposed to say it.

At the beginning of the war—*East Coker* was published in September 1940—the poet had every right to borrow a topical simile from the vocabulary of war, and he used it without a patriotic undertone. He wanted to give precision to an intense moment ('a lifetime burning in every moment'), the kind of precision which escapes between words. For each venture into language, as Eliot says, is 'a raid on the inarticulate/With shabby equipment always deteriorating/In the general mess of imprecision of feeling.'

Since a good poet has to struggle for precision over and over again, his experience of intense moments resembles the surface of a battlefield and not a storehouse filled with labelled past events. Language as experience preoccupies the poet who writes and the poet who has abandoned words, because experience, too, requires precision to become meaningful.

2

Horace in his ode '*Exegi monumentum aere perennius*' launched a theme in which poets over the centuries recognized their professional self-justification. His monument and those they erected one after another had only one durable thing in common: all were built from the material of language. And the material possessed a solidity of experience that could be tested and felt again and again, as long as language continued to be inherited, that is re-experienced.

This is your monument, Shakespeare repeats in his sonnets, giving his lover a Horatian assurance of survival. 'Your monument shall be my gentle verse' (LXXXI). The epithet referring to his verse changes with mood, but not the promise laid 'in eternal lines', which will be read by 'eyes not yet created'. In a short farewell lyric Słowacki uses the image of the monument to withhold, it seems, for ever the transience of parting. For it is 'the poet's brightest glory' to be able to turn a farewell into a statue. 'Centuries will not wipe away these lines.'[1]

Such statements about endurance accord to the material of language a superiority which neither the personal legend of the poet nor the glory of his subject can ever equal. Legends die and lofty subjects tumble down. But the language used by a genius lives on as experience because it perpetuates experience. In this sense perhaps Shelley describes it as 'a perpetual Orphic song'.[2] The emphasis seems right. For it is not the poet, but his language that crosses the domains of death and emerges alive.

The more faith is put in endurance through language, the more syntactic becomes the view of poetic diction. Metaphor, above all, is singled out as a device which keeps words close to the intense moments of experience: metaphor is not just the best words in the best order, but rather experience in the most dynamic syntax. The traditional classifications of metaphor, from Aristotle onwards, have mainly emphasized the genus-species or the animate–inanimate relationships, and on the whole have concentrated on the idea-content rather than on the syntax.[3] For the modern poet, however, metaphoric structure matters more than the subdivisions of its content: it shows language in action and has little to do with any static assortment of verbal embellishments.

When the Argentinian poet Jorge Luis Borges acknowledges

---

[1] Bo to jest wieszcza najjaśniejsza chwała,
Że w posąg mieni nawet pożegnanie.
Ta kartka wieki tu będzie płakała
I łez jej stanie.

[2] *Prometheus Unbound*, Act IV.

[3] See Christine Brooke-Rose, *A Grammar of Metaphor* (London, 1958), chapter I.

metaphor, he sees it as the poet's active thought and not a mere technique of replacement that enhances style. He thinks in metaphors because to formulate metaphors is to think (*'Metaforizar es pensar, es reunir representaciones o ideas'*).[1] But he also stresses the suddenness of such experience, 'an instantaneous contact of two images'; there cannot be a methodical assimilation of two things in a metaphor.[2] The poet therefore projects these sudden mental connexions on to the structure of language which has their potential equivalents. As metaphor is his creative thought, he must probe below the surface reality which language has already mapped out by means of cliché. Wallace Stevens tells us in a neat epigram that 'Reality is a cliché from which we escape by metaphor'.[3]

Should the Borges equation of thought with metaphor seem too facile, we find, in Stevens again, the same emphasis on the function of thought in poetry: 'Accuracy of observation,' he says, 'is the equivalent of accuracy of thinking.'[4] This undoubtedly brings the poet's metaphoric vision near to that of the scientist who sees beyond the accepted cliché of colour and shape. If so, metaphor must imply renewed discovery and can otherwise hardly be expected, on its own, to prolong the life of some static monument, any more than language alone can be *aere perennius*.

3

Borges, quite rightly, insists on the moment of recognition, the sudden contact between images. When Marvell hears 'Time's wingèd chariot hurrying near', he traces a metaphoric connexion, using for this purpose a possessive genitive and a verb. The connexion is valid within the concept of the poem which for all its irony relies on the familiar references to the Bible and the beliefs concerning the end of time and the Last Judgement. Today Marvell's chariot would also have to satisfy our idea of relativity, no matter how imperfect it may be. The metaphoric

---

[1] *'El culteranismo'*. Compare this with *'la metáfora es asunto acostumbrado de mi pensar'* in *'Otra vez la metáfora'*. Both essays are included in *El idioma de los Argentinos* (Buenos Aires, 1928).

[2] '. . . *la metáfora es el contacto momentáneo de dos imágenes, no la metódica asimilación de dos cosas*'. *'Quevedo'* from *Otras inquisiciones* (Buenos Aires, 1960).

[3] 'Adagia', in *Opus Posthumous* (New York, 1957).

[4] Ibid.

potentials of our imagination are closer to the space-ship than to the chariot. Instead of being chased by time, we would rather visualize our interstellar chase of time.

Once metaphor is understood to be the experience of an intense moment or the instantaneous contact of two images, its survival value will depend on the extent to which it can be catalogued, attached to a period or a stylistic convention. The inventor of *greguerías*, Ramón Gómez de la Serna, calls the moon 'a bank of ruined metaphors'.[1] This echoes Marinetti's dismissal of the poets' moonlight: *Tuons le Clair de Lune* is the title of his pamphlet. Perhaps the lunar metaphor will be given a new lease of vitality now that the landing on the moon has become a fact. But because this is fact, the modern imagination can no longer accept the old poetic moonshine: one bank of metaphors is certainly bankrupt.

We are coming back to Eliot's realization in *East Coker* that language, even when treated as experience, has only a provisional validity; and the high claims of Horace, too, belong now to the depository of convention. Metaphors at their best remain uncorrupted by cliché. Structurally, they are scaffoldings around invisible reality, each put up with magical suddenness but liable to vanish under a prosaic scrutiny.

It is not surprising that at the age of twenty-two Borges believed that lyrical poetry should be reduced to its 'primordial element, the metaphor'.[2] Later, during his mature years, he met the challenge of time as a poetic subject. Was the experience of time also reducible to an instant? Could the metaphor really be regarded as the expression of relativity which in the opinion of Gómez de la Serna suited the modern man, 'more oscillating than in any other century and therefore more metaphoric'?[3] Once Borges allowed the fascination with time to grow, the essayist and short-story writer developed in him at the expense of the lyrical poet.[4] He gradually withdrew from writing verse

---

[1] '*La Luna es un banco de metáforas arruinado*', *Greguerías 1940–1945* (Buenos Aires' 1945). In his introduction to this collection Gómez de la Serna defines the *greguería* as humour + metaphor.

[2] The manifesto of *Ultraísmo*, 1921.

[3] *Greguerías 1940–1945*, Introduction. Compare this with Novalis' '*Der Mensch: Metapher*' (*Fragmente*).

[4] The collection *Poemas 1923–1958* (Buenos Aires, 1958) contains very few poems written after 1935. Borges was born in 1899.

because, in my view, he found that lyrical statements tend to be evasive. It is enough to compare his poem about 'the fourth element' ('*Poema del cuarto elemento*') with his treatment of time in his *Historia de la eternidad* (1936) or in the short piece '*La biblioteca de Babel*', to see how much more precisely the prose appears to work.

The universe (which some people call the Library) is composed of an indefinite, and perhaps infinite number of hexagonal galleries. These galleries have vast ventilation wells down the middle, round the edge of which run very low rails. . . . On the wall of each hexagon are five shelves; each shelf contains thirty-two books of uniform size; each book has four hundred and ten pages, each page forty lines and each line, eighty black letters.[1]

The story is remarkable for its visual sequence. Have metaphors perhaps proved to be thoughts out of sequence and thus unsuited to a speculative argument? And the library itself, is it not a metaphoric extension rather than a reduction, similar in its technique of parallel images to the mirror-like effect of allegory? 'In the passage there is a mirror which faithfully doubles appearances. Men usually infer from this mirror that the Library is not infinite (if it really were, why this illusory duplicator?).'

Calderón describes allegory as a mirror (*espejo*). The mirror projects (*translada*) what *is* on to that which *is not*. And he who looks at one of them thinks he is looking at both (*a entrambas*).

> La alegoría no es más
> que un espejo que translada
> lo que es con lo que no es,
> y esta toda su elegancia
> en que salga parecida
> tanto la copia en la tabla
> que el que está mirando a una
> piense que está viendo a entrambas.[2]

The library in the story of Borges becomes a continually repeated parallel, an echoing inside an allegorical mirror which must endure so that we may imagine the limitless pattern of the

---

[1] I quote from G. R. Coulthard's translation, 'The Library of Babel', published in the magazine *Nine* (Winter 1950–51).

[2] *El Verdadero Dios Pan* (1670) (Lawrence, Kans., 1949), verses 509–16.

universe.[1] Like Calderón's explanation of allegory it seems to suggest that all appearances happen *sub specie aeternitatis*. Language has the appearance of experience precisely because appearances matter to us. Is, however, experience nothing but appearances? Both Eliot and Borges lead us to this query as to a point of departure.

4

In his provocative study, *Saving the Appearances*, Owen Barfield discusses the world lost to our modern consciousness, 'a world in which both phenomenon and name were felt as representations.' 'The earlier awareness', he argues,

involved experiencing the phenomena as representations; the latter preoccupation involves experiencing them, non-representationally, as objects in their own right, existing independently of human consciousness. This latter experience, in its extreme form, I have called *idolatry*.[2]

Barfield shows how man is trying to eliminate all original participation, how meaning is removed from his language, undermining his collective representations. And the knowledge of nature is progressively fragmented, his science 'is losing its grip on any principle of unity pervading nature as a whole'.[3]

In view of what I have said about metaphor and its structural function in the poet's language, it is important to understand the unifying urge behind all metaphoric links. It is as if metaphor were designed to 'save the appearances', to restore something of the lost participation.[4] Hence its instantaneous structures, bold leaps over a deep precipice, from one image to another—a sudden recognition of unity is revealed, but the

---

[1] This is how 'The Library of Babel' ends: 'If an eternal traveller crossed it in any direction, he would discover at the end of centuries that the same volumes are repeated in the same disorder (which, repeated, would be an order: the Order). My loneliness is cheered by this elegant hope.'

[2] *Saving the Appearances* (London, 1957), chapter XXI. It is worth recalling the analogous views of Herder on the integral intuition of early man. There was no division in his perception.

[3] Ibid.

[4] In an article 'The Riddle of the Sphinx', contributed to a symposium on semantics in *Arena* (April 1964), Owen Barfield wrote: 'For the *pons asinorum* of etymology is the discovery that the meaning of virtually every word we use can be traced back to a time when it had a metaphorical or at all events a figurative significance.'

very act of revelation seems to illuminate the vast areas of fragmented experience, of phenomena detached from their original representation. 'A heap of broken images' in Eliot's waste land describes not only the desolation but also the hankering after a unified pattern.

One begins to sympathize with the passion for metaphor as a new philosopher's stone, *lapis philosophorum* from the language of alchemy. Borges in his 'Ultraist' youth wanted to reach to the centre of appearances, all surface values had to be discarded, and he thought he had found the centre in 'the primordial metaphor'. But he also said that true metaphors which formulate hidden (*intímos*) connexions between one image and another have always existed. If he really believed that one could not invent primordial metaphors, he must have meant much the same as Barfield when he speaks of the lost sense of participation.

Perhaps for this reason also Borges found metaphor as instantaneous contact unsatisfactory, once he began to probe the meaning of time. The appearances could not be fully reclaimed for modern poetry, hence the decision to abandon verse in order to perfect the common speech of prose.

When Eliot meditates in *East Coker* on the intense moment of experience, it is for him an act of momentary partaking which only confirms that full participation cannot be attained. Whatever language appropriates through someone's experience, remains its gain, but all such gains, no matter how large their sum total, do not seem to have recovered the lost area of *original* participation. Words do not become things in the process of appropriation. And though language may at times be identical with experience, poets find it hard to believe that this is their paradise regained, their final refuge.

CHAPTER V

THE WITNESSES

I

I am writing this chapter partly as a witness. It concerns a Polish literary movement which in the late thirties began to be known as *autentyzm*. About ten poets were associated with it and printed their work in the monthly *Okolica Poetów* (The Poets' Neighbourhood), which was founded in 1935 by Stanisław Czernik, poet and theoretician of the movement. He was then thirty-six, the oldest of the group; most of the others were barely twenty or even younger. The monthly appeared in a small provincial town.[1] Its contributors, however, came from different parts of Poland, and each poet-*autentysta* had strong regional ties, openly professing his distrust of metropolitan culture.

In fact, among these practitioners of poetic authenticity three were, like myself, of peasant origin and regarded themselves, perhaps too self-consciously at times, as exiles from the village, forced to seek intellectual work in the town. They all wanted to bear witness to concrete and minute realities of their immediate surroundings. In their childhood memories, too, they emphasized the small but verifiable world of objects. This process of witnessing resulted in the frequent use of proper names, place-names, dates, specific dialect terms, and so on. Although the movement was soon to be interrupted by the war, it managed to establish itself in the modern Polish tradition and is now being studied.

Autentyzm happened at the right time. The circumstances, both social and literary, were in favour of a native theory that would penetrate below the urban surface down to the roots of a common culture. Poland had entered the second decade of independence, it was still predominantly agricultural, but from its overpopulated villages there began to emerge a new type of intellectual, educated in the state schools and universities. The

[1] Ostrzeszów Wielkopolski in western Poland, where Czernik was a teacher in a secondary school.

first free generation produced a social pattern which could not remain dominated by the intelligentsia for much longer. It was up to these newcomers from the villages to redress the political loss of face, which the peasant parliamentarians suffered in the military *coup d'état* of May 1926. A peasant intellectual had to assert himself. If he was a poet, he needed the support of a literary theory rather than the applause of the intelligentsia who would out of habit treat him as a freak.[1]

A parallel social phenomenon arose in England after the last war when writers of working-class origin entered the literary scene equipped with the higher education which the modern state had given them free. They were more sophisticated and self-assured than their predecessors in the thirties, who only too often spoilt their social realism with naïve black-and-white propaganda. One of the results of this new class consciousness has been the predominance of themes from the recent past rather than from the present, prompted not only by childhood memories but also by the artistic desire to change the manner and tone previously associated with proletarian writing. Social indignation, it would seem, is never quite up to date because the causes of any such indignation are better described by the next generation.

In form, Polish *autentyzm* developed from the literary *avant-garde* which had absorbed the Futurist cult of machines, modern speed, and violent reportage. With it came the euphoria of metaphor, the attack on syntax, punctuation, and capital letters. The Polish *avant-garde* poets of the late twenties and early thirties[2] adhered to the urban bias of the Futurists; some of them wrote earnest poems about factories, electrification, and coal mines. Soon, however, the strain of keeping up with the imported theories began to show, the adulation of the universal multi-town looked grotesque next to the familiar and provincial realities of the country as a whole.

The metaphoric language, too, became mechanically repetitive by linking nouns at random. It produced combinations like 'the engine of the night', 'the stockings of the street', and

---

[1] Even Jan Kasprowicz, the first great Polish poet of peasant origin, was accorded this puzzled treatment by some of his ardent admirers. Kasprowicz was born in 1860 and died in 1926, nine years before *autentyzm* began.

[2] *Awangarda* was, in fact, the term applied to the experimental poetry of that period.

'the loaves of sunlight'. This was *fantazjotwórstwo*, a mere patch-work of fantasy, to use a term which recurred in theoretical articles on *autentyzm*. Hence the insistence that metaphor, a complex one especially, should correspond to its equivalent in experience. The smaller the experience, the *autentysta* would say, the harder for a poetic lie to pass unnoticed. A poem is authentic when it is verifiable, not just in the mood or sentiment it arouses, but throughout the text, at every stage of its original growth.

There was no difficulty with the provincial subject-matter which could be tested against the observable facts. But the young provincials who wrote about it did not assume it was all that familiar. On the contrary, they showed again and again how a concrete detail would appear new to the eye, even exotic, once it was given its full due. Giving the details their full due seemed to be the simplest explanation of what *autentyzm* was trying to do.

> My poem is just such a small church among nettles:
> a black clay bottle on the brick wall.[1]

The point about a statement like this is that it does not make a religious comparison or any other emotional valuation. The objects placed next to one another, the church, the brick wall, and the clay bottle, are different in size, incongruous perhaps when compared, but they are there, a visual event which this poem accepts. Nothing else is required of it, because the authentic equivalents can stand on their own, they are meant to be independent.

When the mood is close to a childhood recollection, it is close to sentiment: a village boy, for instance, tending horses. Yet here, too, the memory keeps a shrewd eye on detail. The result is nearer to the child's wit than to that of the adult gazing at the past:

> It is me shoving cherries up into the sun's mouth.
> And a frog, hanging from the sunflower,
>   looks after the horses.[2]

Both quotations come from Ożóg's first book of verse, *Wyjazd wnuka* (The Grandson's Departure). Ożóg was born the son of a village organist and studied to be a priest, but found he had no

---

[1] J. B. Ożóg, '*Poezja*', from the volume *Wyjazd wnuka* (Ostrzeszów Wielkopolski, 1937).   [2] '*Z rana*' (In the Morning), op. cit.

vocation, left the seminary for the university and became a writer. He fought in the Underground Army during the occupation, survived the war, and despite the pressure of socialist realism has remained faithful to *autentyzm*.

After thirty years his first volume strikes one still with its original freshness which comes from the diversity and treatment of detail. The courtyard, the cottage, the church, the journey in a cart or on a bicycle, the seminarist's anxiety—each reality yields its details in abundance. The choice and the fidelity to the chosen object is what matters above all. An occasional clumsiness seems to increase the sense of being inside the poet's workshop. One watches him struggling with the rough and awkward shapes to find words that would suit them and not smooth out the irregularity of life. Ożóg keeps these rough edges and rarely allows an emotion to heal an incident which must have caused him pain. This is how he relates the death of a bird which happened during a bicycle ride:

> Into the silver spokes of my bicycle
> a little swallow flew.
> I arrive with a red wheel
> for the bird-cherry taking the veil.[1]

The death is not sentimentalized over, only stated. He did not, after all, see the exact moment of the swallow falling between the spokes; he saw the bloodstains on arrival against the white of the bird-cherry (*czeremcha*). The act of witnessing concerns the facts as much as the sequence in which they occurred. Even the juxtaposition of colour has no special function beyond being recorded: this is not a baroque concept, something that ought to be striking, but an event that strikes us as true.

Here is a passage about a human tragedy. Józef Andrzej Frasik, another *autentysta*, describes the death of his sister:

> At dawn when the candles went out and the sparrows knocked
>   at the window,
> Mother hid her huge weeping in her apron.
> The old women taking milk to town, crossed a brother's way.
> 'Is she dead?' (The cart drivers on the road were cracking their
>   whips hard.)[2]

---

[1] '*Krew na srebrnym kole*' (Blood on the Silver Wheel), op. cit.
[2] The last stanza from '*Pożegnanie siostry*' (Farewell to Sister) in Frasik's first book of verse, *Łąkami w górę* (Upwards through the Meadows) (Cracow, 1936).

The cool phrase in brackets achieves its purpose. The detail is right.

While pursuing truth in the minute manifestations of life, the poet-*autentysta* had a justified hope that being minute they could at least be apprehended, if not understood. For him witnessing came always before understanding. 'Here you can place life in the palm of your hand,' Frasik wrote about a small town; 'at dusk the old troubles/Go with sledge-bells to the fields of snow nearby.'[1]

When, however, real people and real place names were involved, the business of verification by the reader could become dangerous for the author. My own poem, *Prowincja*, was serialized in a popular literary weekly, then published in book form (1936). It told a number of interwoven stories, each scene being set in an existing place, the name of each character authentic. All of them came from the same region, the land of Dobrzyn.[2]

A few months after the publication of *Prowincja* I happened to be in the same village I had used as the setting for a harvest festival in the poem. The occasion was the feast of harvest again. But this time a rich farmer whose name was mentioned in the poem gave me a good chase in the moonlight right across a large stubble field. A character was in pursuit of the author with the intention of giving him a rough lesson in authenticity. Being much younger than he, I escaped. Oddly enough, *Prowincja* contained a passage about someone running across a moonlit field, but there the coincidence ended.

Now I cannot help thinking that the character who frightened the author in me, gave in practice the best possible verification of *autentyzm*.

2

A new literary theory has always two facets. One is consciously displayed and manifests confidence, the other is hidden and almost frightened of itself. The same was true of *autentyzm* from the very beginning. It had to be defined, exemplified, arranged into a system so that potential heretics could not pull it to pieces. Czernik was busy writing theoretical articles in *Okolica Poetów*

---

[1] '*Zima w miasteczku*' (Winter in a Small Town), op. cit.
[2] Close to the lake belt on the right side of the Vistula, to the west of Torun.

and encouraging his first apostles. He had a really good idea
when he asked his contributors to write very frank answers on
the subject, 'How the poem is created'. The results were important for *autentyzm* at that stage: it now had a few versions of
its own creed and genesis from the first practitioners of the
movement. What they said in their replies to the questionnaire
sounded sometimes naïve and earnest, nevertheless it was the
raw material on which good criticism could be founded.

The hidden facet of *autentyzm* lived in each individual poet
who belonged to the movement. It had unrecognizable features
distorted by fear, and this fear showed itself on the surface in
conventional bogeys and slogans. The poets wrote how frightened
they were of the urban monster the metropolis—poor village
innocents lost in the stone forest full of noises. Cosmopolitan
culture and the town meant the same, and from neither could
vision ever come. Even if it were true that all highways led to
the metropolis, poetry still lay by the side of a village road.

In its disavowal of cosmopolitan, that is urban culture, the
early *autentyzm* echoed the pastoral protests of the sixteenth and
the seventeenth centuries, directed against court and town.
And it had another thing in common with those protests: its
anti-urban voice, like theirs, expressed, in fact, a fascination
with the wicked town, and the fascination was understandable.

Now, the hidden fear which the poet-*autentysta* had yet no
courage to name pointed to the future, not to the past. In
bleared confused shapes he saw a catastrophe ahead of him, the
end of the rural civilization. In Poland before 1939 this seemed
an unfounded anxiety, and for the *autentysta* an odd prophecy to
intercept. There he was, officially proclaiming the recognition
of his provincial uniqueness, and underneath he sensed a death-
warrant in that uniqueness. Was he authentic because he
wanted to rejoice in the multiplying diversity of things, or, on
the contrary, was he authentic because he had to bear witness
and record the vanishing village world?

Ożóg wrote a poem about Esenin.[1] This was not unusual.
Esenin appealed to most Polish poets of Ożóg's generation.
What made it different, however, was the feeling of identifica-
tion: Esenin had seen the threat to a rural Russia which the
Soviet state later put into practice. Ożóg did not and could not

---

[1] '*Do Jesienina*', from his first book, *Wyjazd wnuka*.

tell at that time how the threat would become a reality in his country.

Willy-nilly, *autentyzm* began to grope among the concrete events and objects for something which was distant and not at all verifiable. The war came and suspended all such premonitions for the duration of more imminent perils. Little changed in the provincial realities; objects remained while people were deported and killed. In the end it was Warsaw the metropolis which suffered total destruction. The country had its head severed and left unburied for many witnesses to see.

At first the provincial ethos of *autentyzm* looked oddly out of place in post-war Poland. Frontiers had been brutally altered, causing a mass movement of population; regional identities changed or shifted, the collectivization of farms began, and the pressure of a political canon was applied to all writing.

From time to time, Ożóg stood up for the ignored or forgotten values of *autentyzm*. He never, in fact, disclaimed his allegiance to the movement. This was undoubtedly a dignified behaviour in those days of absurd denunciations and constant bullying. Later, after 1956, Frasik could plainly say what it meant to use themes which were held suspect because of their affinity to the pastoral tradition:

> Since I am of the idyll, they sat in council and pronounced:
> Oh, well, just an idyll—
> so help me, beloved Virgil,
> to gulp wine from the jug.
> Let us invite Theocritus
> and together read idylls with wine.
> . . . .
> My muse was not for the steel of men and for dithyrambs,
> it didn't put Jove's anger into iambics.
> Let other poets praise the brisk flow of history.
> A different wind has blown in,
> and nothing is left of their verses,
> Lethe now is taking care to hide them.[1]

Using the pastoral manner, Frasik makes a political statement. He points at the eulogists of Stalin, who hurriedly commended their poems to oblivion, once the dead dictator was de-canonized at the Kremlin.

[1] '*Wino*' (Wine) from Frasik's volume *Śpiewny czas* (The Singing Time) (Cracow, 1957).

The official policy towards the peasant writer in the People's Republic was, to say the least, ambiguous, and has remained so until the present day. Phoney folklore for export is preferred to genuine regional culture. A jumping peasant, *sclavus saltans*, in some *ballet-monstre* on permanent tour is supposed to represent the happy village of today. And this looks like an almost wilful mockery of authenticity. Individual artists of peasant origin are given far less encouragement than one would legitimately expect in a country where even after the process of industrialization 50 per cent of the population is rural.[1] Modern Polish culture has remained predominantly middle-class, with a few aristocratic adornments.

For better or worse, *autentyzm* is the poetry of witnessing, and now it has the task of recording the decay of the Polish village. As in the history of the pastoral *genre*, the idyll has once again turned into an elegy.

3

In 1958 Stanisław Piętak published a poem about a wedding in a present-day village. The wedding seems to have become an obsessive formula in Polish literature, attracting both myth and social comment.[2] So it is with Piętak:

> The music-band went on tugging, inviting to the circle,
> and yet the village appeared to be dead.
> The empty street, empty square, empty fields;
> the tired silence spread round like a whisper.
> No, there is no joy, that joy which was here.
> No old men talking things over on footbridges, thresholds, in
>   windows.
> No children racing one another in orchards, on green plots.
> The night flies in, will touch the empty place with pain.[3]

From this one particular occasion there gapes the whole modern exodus from villages to towns. Like a medieval plague

---

[1] The superb irony is that the zealots of social realism denounced the pioneers of peasant writing, the novelist Reymont and the poet Kasprowicz.

[2] Wyspiański's symbolist play *Wesele* set the tone in 1901 and influenced a number of writers, the latest example being Sławomir Mrożek, as in *Zabawa* and *Tango*.

[3] '*Wesele*' (VI), from the volume *Szczęście i cierpienie* (Happiness and Suffering) (Cracow, 1958). Piętak (1909–1964), though never a declared follower of *autentyzm*, was very close to the movement and published his poems in *Okolica Poetów*. His style reveals all the characteristic features of *autentyzm*.

it left the ghosts of cottages and a desolated landscape. Ożóg's bicycle is a thing of the past. It was succeeded by the noisy motorcycle which at once reduced the distance to big towns, and the provinces began to look like suburbs.

The deserted village is a new theme in Polish poetry, but not in English. Goldsmith recalled the rural life as it used to be before the Enclosures Act and 'stern depopulation'. The date of his poetic requiem is 1770.

> The noisy geese that gabbled o'er the pool,
> The playful children just let loose from school;
> The watchdog's voice that bay'd the whisp'ring wind,
> And the loud laugh that spoke the vacant mind:
> These all in sweet confusion sought the shade,
> And filled each pause the nightingale had made.[1]

A later eighteenth-century poet, George Crabbe, looked at the poor of the village and understood how very ineffectual pastoral complaints were. His muse grimaced with irony over his own accomplished verses:

> To you the smoothest song is smooth in vain;
> O'ercome by labour, and bow'd down by time,
> Feel you the barren flattery of a rhyme?
> Can poets soothe you, when you pine for bread,
> By winding myrtles round your ruin'd shed?[2]

The decline of rural communities was the price most West European countries were prepared to pay for industrialization and material progress. The erosion of cultural resources hardly caused concern. When the process hit Poland after the war, at the lowest point of national strength, the sense of danger was felt, and the poets of *autentyzm* reacted to it in much the same way, though independently of one another. Both their social instinct and their ability to see the authentic detail equipped them for this task of witnessing and recording.

'The empty village' became their common theme. Ożóg gave this title to a poem which he significantly dedicated to Piętak.

> Where the carts are overgrown with grass,
> a flower of chicory next to a stone,
> and over the stone is it the sky's flower
> or a cloud down to the knees of a birch? . . .

---

[1] *The Deserted Village*, verses 119–24.   [2] *The Village* (1783), Book I.

The poem ends with these lines:

> And the bird goes to sleep alone.
> The ossuary stands on the village threshold.[1]

Town-peasants are a new social class with no sense of belonging anywhere. They still try to help those who have stayed behind. Ożóg speaks for them, for their uprooted and baffled thoughts:

> Why when we take a parcel to the post-office,
>   does it never arrive in time for the living?
> And the neighbours dress the empty rooms,
>   and in our well-worn jackets
>   they lower fathers into the oak coffins.[2]

There is anger in Ożóg's voice and pain from the wounded pride which he shares with all peasants.

> But a bold peasantry, their country's pride,
> When once destroy'd, can never be supplied.[3]

Two hundred years after Goldsmith, the warning has almost become a verifiable fact. There is just such an obsession with visual verification in the repeated returns to the native house, which both Piętak and Ożóg use as a separate theme.

> The landscape is so familiar it is almost dark,
>   whether I go out to the cross-roads
>   or stand under the plum or the pear-tree,
>   to which I snuggled long ago.
> On my knees I want to embrace this patch
>   where the window threw light from father's house
>   and played with the darkness and the shudder of trees.
> They all avoid me, they don't recognize me,
>   so I walk alone, a stranger,
>   so I run,
>   in the belief that I must have arrived years too early or years
>   too late.[4]

In consuming each particular experience this obsession makes it impersonal, and the concrete detail loses its authentic claim on

---

[1] '*Pusta wieś*' (The Empty Village), from the volume *Gdzie powój woła* (Where the Ivy Calls) (Cracow, 1961).

[2] '*Nowi*' (The New Ones), op. cit.

[3] Goldsmith, *The Deserted Village*, verses 55–6.

[4] From Piętak's last book of verse, *Zaklinania* (Spells) (Warsaw, 1963). The poem has no title.

reality. This happened to Ożóg in his later verse. Even his conscious recollection of the same objects as in his first book gives them an air of uncertainty, they seem dislodged from their natural habitat. Ożóg appears to be far less exact, as if he did not care much about precision in observation when the village world seems condemned to die. This is clear in poems like '*Kiedy*' (When). The 'when' spells inevitable doom:

> When there is no more soil in window boxes
> for the fields of wheat
> and the towns begin to choke
> beside the streams and sources of the earth,
> covered with the pillow of iron.[1]

For the Virgilian Frasik the passing of the Golden Age is perennial: it vanishes with childhood. Perhaps the peasantry, too, is letting its civilization go because it can no longer hold to the memory of its childhood. *Autentyzm* may have been once beautifully naïve, but it has now learnt the pain of its own sophistication. What was static, verifiable and safe has become relative, and the horizons are on the move all the time.

Is the poet-*autentysta* today a man broken by the task of witnessing? Ożóg sees him like that. His poem '*Autentyści*' comes at the end of *Poezje wybrane*, a large selection of his verse, and reads like the farewell of a haunted man. From the first lines a vocabulary of *knives*, *venom*, *vipers*, *wounds* leads to the stanza:

> A broken jug, a green jug,
> crushed and glued up together,
> that's you, that's me.

The poem ends:

> It is worse and it is more difficult
> to speak in blood of the greenery.[2]

The poet-*autentysta* began by bearing witness to the visible world; he took each experience to be a microcosm, his vision was firmly grounded, and the prophet's leap[3] did not tempt him. Perhaps in the very smallness and modesty of his search

---

[1] From the collection *Żywioł* (Element) in *Poezje wybrane* (Cracow, 1965).

[2] Ibid. In an introspective poem '*Kim jestem*' (Who am I) Ożóg wrote the line: 'I—a patient in a home for the mentally sick.'

[3] See chapter IX.

lay the truth whose size was likened in a parable[1] to a grain of mustard seed.

He arrived at the opposite of his intention: his imagination was shown the expanding emptiness of the village world about to perish. He now had to witness the death of his authentic detail, and with it the death of his poetry.

Stanisław Piętak committed suicide in January 1964. His last book of poems is charged with premonitions, it is a testament of sickness and a prologue to death. One poem, in particular, reads like a post-mortem on *autentyzm*. It shows the workings of an imagination which has penetrated the microcosm of objects, and now must try to fight them back as they become menacing. The title of the poem is also that of the whole book, *Zaklinania* (Spells):

> Again they have come to life, my old things,
> and take pity on me or darkly sneer at me.
> . . . .
> You have so little room now, but it will be enough
> for you to kneel or fall down,
> to shout, curse and weep.
> We have taken your pen—still you know how to write
> on sand with your finger, in sleep with your moan.[2]

One knows as one reads the poem that the battle will be lost. The spells of magic and counter-magic do not work for the poet-*autentysta*. And he cannot escape into prophecy which someone else might verify or refute in a distant future. He remains a witness, even when he is recording his own defeat.

[1] Matthew, 13.
[2] *Zaklinania*, op. cit. The poem itself may allude to the feeling of entrapment, experienced in a mental home.

CHAPTER VI

THE ROBOTS AND THE LILIES
OF THE FIELD

I

Surrounded by things, we may at first see them as sentries placed about our magic circle: this is the child's protective vision. During adolescence and maturity, however, the sense of being separated from things grows with acquired knowledge, whether tested by particular experience or not. Environment is more than society to which one has to adjust oneself; it is also a world of things, a permanent exhibition of still life where our adjustment would serve no purpose. Things remain separate, the possibility of any participation seems both remote and unsympathetic.

It is here that Rilke's challenge of things (*Dinge*) has special relevance to the poet's fate. Is he to respect and praise the separateness of things, or is he to remove the barriers and enter into the mute otherness at the risk of disembodying his voice?

We are told that Rilke was advised by the sculptor Rodin to look well at things, not just at their surface appearance but also into their nature.[1] On such close examination they would yield something of their independent existence and seem more tangible by attracting the observer's sympathy. Rilke has left many records of this repeated attempt to penetrate the nature of *Dinge*. The most revealing statement, however, is to be found in a short poem about his own identity being used up to enrich the identity of things. The piece is called simply '*Der Dichter*' (The Poet). Only eight lines long, it manages to convey the sense of vulnerable isolation: the poet has neither a belovèd nor a home, nor even a place in which to live; yet he has given

---

[1] In *Auguste Rodin*, a lecture delivered in 1907, Rilke speaks at length about the *Dinge*. Here is a typical remark: 'Ein Ding nachformen, das hiess: über jede Stelle gegangen sein, nichts verschwiegen, nichts übersehen, nirgends betrogen haben; alle die hundert Profile kennen, alle die Aufsichten und Untersichten, jede Überschneidung.'

himself to the things that are around him. This is the second stanza:

> Ich habe keine Geliebte, kein Haus,
> keine Stelle, auf der ich lebe.
> Alle Dinge, an die ich mich gebe,
> werden reich und geben mich aus.

The things are made rich by the poet, and the poet in turn is expended by the things he has enriched. The paradox of giving is balanced here on the grammatical repetition: the pronoun *mich* occurs in two opposite contexts and so does the verb *geben*, which withholds its second meaning until the prefix *aus* comes at the very end. In spending himself on the multitude of things, Rilke's poet resembles the poet whom Keats describes as having no identity.[1] They both accept rather than try to justify the risk of exchanging one identity for many as yet unspecified.

This situation is essentially different from that in which the Baroque poets identify objects, precious, glittering, quaint, or grotesque. These come arranged in a collection, set like stones into the jewel of a concept; they always serve a purpose, and on occasion may appear to furnish the poet's own self, as if it were a luxurious bower. A seventeenth-century Pole, Twardowski, knows how to look at the objects of nature through the work-manship of man. He describes the crowd in the mosque at Istanbul:

> Tall turbaned heads, bright caftans in the choir,
> And togas, silken, shimmering like flame,
> Workmanship various as the tongue can name.
> Not shapes of sea-shells on a shore of sand,
> Their patterns whittled by sly nature's hand,
> Nor shades of tulips from a myriad buds
> Drowning whole valleys under fragrant floods,
> Could more delight. The Emperor sat down,
> A silent populace stilled at his frown.[2]

The Spaniard Góngora takes a rhetorical deep breath each time he is about to astonish us with splendour in *Soledades* or

---

[1] 'A Poet is the most unpoetical of any thing in existence; because he has no Identity. . . .' Letter to Richard Woodhouse, 17 October 1818.

[2] From *Przeważna legacja* . . . (The Most Important Embassy), 1633. The extract in English is from *Five Centuries of Polish Poetry*, op. cit. Samuel Twardowski wrote two long epic poems and pastoral romances.

in his sonnets. Ivory, marble, ebony, amber, gold, silver, crystal, pearls, sapphires, rubies—the lines are studded with riches:

> Cual del Ganges marfil, o cual de Paro
> blanco mármol, cual ébano luciente,
> cual ámbar rubio o cual oro excelente,
> cual fina plata o cual cristal tan claro,
> cual tan menudo aljófar, cual tan caro
> oriental safir, cual rubí ardiente. . . .[1]

A collection of things like this belongs to the inventory of man, he has domesticated nature, bits of stone and metal, their glitter and touch.

An eighteenth-century poet, William Cowper, proves in *The Task* that nature can be tamed further. The comforts indoors and the pleasures out of doors are there for man to appreciate; the sofa mediates between them, an object and a subject.

> But relaxation of the languid frame
> By soft recumbency of outstretched limbs,
> Was bliss reserved for happier days;—so slow
> The growth of what is excellent, so hard
> To attain perfection in this nether world.
> Thus first necessity invented stools,
> Convenience next suggested elbow chairs,
> And luxury the accomplished sofa last.[2]

This taming of things has much to commend it: the homely muse, whether classical or romantic, accepts the *status quo*. Mickiewicz, for instance, glorifies domesticity in his epic *Pan Tadeusz*; he can give a catalogue of mushrooms and play on their native names (Book III) without in any sense detracting from the romantic irony which permeates the human relationships. This irony, unlike the classical, depends on mutability, yet it does not affect things which are still regarded as obedient

---

[1] '*Cual del Ganges marfil . . .*' is the opening line of this sonnet, in which Luis de Góngora imitates Ariosto's concept. As a contrast, I quote an example of Rilke's *Einsehen* (seeing into) in a parallel subject:

> Ruhig, ruhig, ruf nicht so, Rubin!
> Diese Perle leidet, und es fluten
> Wassertiefen im Aquamarin
>
> ('*Der Goldschmied*' from *Letzte Gedichte*)

[2] *The Task*, Book I. 'The Sofa'.

servants to man their master. He can make use of them, ignore them altogether, or dispose of them, but neither in the eighteenth nor in the nineteenth century does he feel any need to escape from them.

When this possibility occurs, it indicates that things are on the march, threatening to become independent. A new word appears to express this threat: *robot*. It was launched by the twentieth-century Czech writer Karel Čapek.[1] The robot represents a mechanical super-thing, capable, in fact, of developing a psyche of its own.

One form of depression typical of our age is the sensation of being overcome by things. A claustrophobia caused by objects seems to affect both the passive observer and the active cataloguer, the latter trying hard to be in charge. But the man responsible for the inventory no longer feels he is above things, he cannot claim to be their absolute master. And so their presence becomes oppressive: one wants to escape.

Rilke faced the problem by admitting a possibility of relationships with the *Dinge*. To observe them as independent entities meant to recognize them for their own sake. The result would be some form of empathy which would enable one to enter into the nature of things. Hence Rilke's realization in '*Der Dichter*' that the poet is enriching things while they are partaking of him. As in love, the generosity of giving matters more than reciprocation which in any case can hardly be expected from an inanimate object.

2

In the process of knowing things, adjectives like 'tangible' and 'superficial' acquire new meanings. There is a superficial way of glancing at them and there is also the experience of the surface through the sense of touch. To some a tangible object seems to reveal its essence. A shape or texture may be felt much as the sense imparted by a word or phrase is felt. Maria Konopnicka, a prolific and on the whole disappointing poetess, has left a memorable description of this tangible sensation in a poem

---

[1] The live robots (from *robota*—labour, servitude) in Čapek's play *R.U.R* (1921) reproduce and revolt against man. There is an English study of Čapek by William E. Harkins (New York, 1962).

about Cicero: 'His hands moving along the Etruscan vase,/He learnt how to enclose its round shape within words'.[1]

This is exactly what Rilke was later trying to define with precision, whether his objects were inanimate as in *'Das Portal'* or animals like *'Der Panther'* and *'Der Hund'*. The tangible world can be an embraceable world, warm and intensified by man spiritually: a thing may reveal itself to us as 'happy, innocent and therefore ours', but not in the sense of being possessed by us. *'Wie glücklich ein Ding sein kann, wie schuldlos und unser.'*[2]

In the Ninth Elegy of the Duino cycle Rilke commends the world of things to the Angel: *'Preise dem Engel die Welt'*—they must be praised before the spirit who is not tangible and cannot be enriched. The angel exists above things; to man he may sometimes appear as a terrible entity, the terror resulting, in fact, from his impenetrable essence. He is, however, 'that Being in whom the transmutation of the Visible into the Invisible is consummated'.[3] Turning to him was a logical step for the poet who had spent his spiritual energy on the things he had learnt to know: from things and animals he moved to a being higher than man. First he had to become poor in spirit so that he could feel the presence of the angel. Nothing tangible in this experience. Because it is rare for men and angels to embrace one another as they do in Botticelli's *Nativity*.

Since Rilke, however, this attitude to objects has changed, in films and novels noticeably more than in recent poetry. The modern poet is made conscious of the impenetrability of things. He need not be a perfectionist of detail, a Keats or a Hopkins opening up a landscape with inscape. A film, a documentary, a snapshot will confirm what he has been brought up to accept: that the perpetually recordable world is none the less independent in every observable detail and harder to penetrate than the intuitive artists had imagined. The French novelist, Alain

---

[1] Tu wodząc miękką dłonią po etruskiej wazie,
    Uczył się jej okrągłość zamykać w wyrazie.
  'W zatoce Baji', from *Italia* (Warsaw, 1901), Konopnicka's best collection of lyrical verse.

[2] *'Die neunte Elegie'*. In *Ur-Geräusch* (1919) Rilke speculates on the possibility of experiencing objects fully, i.e. with each of the five senses. For the artist has *'diese fünffingrige Hand seiner Sinne.'*

[3] Letter to W. Hulewicz, 13 February 1925, from *Selected Letters of Rainer Maria Rilke*, translated by R. F. C. Hull (London, 1946).

Robbe-Grillet, has put this viewpoint most forcefully in several of his essays:

Drowned in the *depth* of things, in the end man doesn't even see them any more; his role is soon limited to feeling, in their name, entirely *humanised* impressions and desires. . . . To describe things, in fact, is deliberately to place oneself outside them, facing them. It is not, any longer, to appropriate them to oneself nor to transfer anything to them. . . . Science is the only honest means at man's disposal whereby he can make use of the world around him—but only material use. . . . Only science, though, can claim to know the *inside* of things. The information about the inside of the pebble, the tree or the snail that Francis Ponge gives us, cares nothing for science. . . . It in no way describes what really is *inside* these things, but merely that part of man's mind that he projects into them.[1]

Robbe-Grillet is against the Rilke type of empathy, against 'the idea of interiorness' which, he says in the same essay, 'always leads to that of transcendence'—and indeed, as we have seen, this is just what it did with Rilke and his angels. Above all, Robbe-Grillet is against the pathetic fallacy which, in our time, has slowly brought about the 'tragification of the universe', either in the form of despair at the discovery that the external world does not after all contain the human meaningfulness with which it has been invested, or in the form of a cynical acceptance that this world is meaningless and therefore absurd.

But the world is neither meaningful nor absurd. It quite simply *is*. And that, in any case, is what is most remarkable about it. . . . All around us, defying our pack of animistic or domesticating adjectives, things *are there*.[2]

This stand of Robbe-Grillet against humanizing metaphors and for the natural object uninvested with human emotions curiously echoes that of Ezra Pound who, already in 1913, was saying:

Don't use such an expression as 'dim lands of *peace*'. It dulls the image. It mixes an abstraction with the concrete. It comes from the writer's not realising that the natural object is always the *adequate* symbol.[3]

[1] 'Nature, Humanism and Tragedy' (1958) from *Snapshots and Towards a New Novel*, translated by Barbara Wright (London, 1965).
[2] 'A Path for the Future Novel' (1956), op. cit.
[3] 'A Few Dont's', from *Poetry*, March 1913, reprinted in *Literary Essays of Ezra Pound*, op. cit.

There is nevertheless an ultimate inconsistency in Robbe-Grillet's position, since his particular technique, based on the formal analogies between things, not only achieves an effect similar to that achieved by metaphor (which he rejects), but also, in its intensity, makes his poetic novels in fact throb with the reflected emotion in the perceiving mind that sees the things.[1] Rilke is more consistent within his own terms, but the problem remains. 'Man looks at the world, but the world does not look back at him.'[2]

3

There is something unresolved in the one-sided relationship with things. If they are to us, as Rilke seems to imply, innocent and happy, perhaps we should move a step further in this spiritual probing and become to the things what they have become to us. Kierkegaard takes up one of Christ's examples from St. Matthew's gospel (6: 28) and suggests: 'Let us consider the lilies and the birds as teachers,' for 'in nature all is unconditional obedience'.[3] This is both a poetic and a moral reversal of the situation. The silence and the separateness of things, whether growing or flying, may have a purpose indirectly relevant to our destiny.

In his adoration of nature, the poet finds an obstacle: the obstacle is of the same kind as in any pantheistic concept of God. If deity is so widely and diversely represented in things, why should we feel the mystical thirst for the void, that is for the absence of natural phenomena?—why should there be a desire to opt out of the tangible and visible universe? Kierkegaard out of respect for the human experience of anxiety and nothingness reminds us how particular Christ is in choosing examples from the human environment. The reference to the lilies and the birds contains a truth applicable to daily life: they teach us not only the beauty of things (the '*hermosura de las cosas*' for St. John of the Cross), but also the meaning of obedience. In nature all is unconditional obedience. A lily-robot or a

[1] See Christine Brooke-Rose, 'The Baroque Imagination of Robbe-Grillet', in *Modern Fiction Studies* (Lafayette, Ind.), XI, 4 (Winter 1965–6).

[2] Robbe-Grillet, 'Nature, Humanism and Tragedy', op. cit.

[3] Søren Kierkegaard, 'The lilies of the field and the birds of the air' (1849) in *Christian Discourses*, translated by Walter Lowrie (New York, 1961).

bird-robot might perhaps challenge this statement. A robot, Karel Čapek has told us, can be equipped with the ability to disobey. Between the real lilies and the robots stands the poet,[1] his identity threatened or used up, his future almost attracting ultimate failure.

Two possibilities present themselves. The first can be likened to the sorcerer's apprentice. By using the magician's wand the apprentice orders the brooms to carry buckets full of water. Once set in motion, the brooms cannot stop and the place is flooded. The second possibility rests in the field of lilies: to accept their obedience and their silence. 'And silent before God like the lily and the bird thou shalt become.'[2]

[1] The poet is, in fact, very much present in Kierkegaard's discourse about the lilies of the field.

[2] Kierkegaard, op. cit.

CHAPTER VII

SILENCE

I

Elected silence is no doubt creative for a Trappist monk. The late Thomas Merton, a monk and a poet, wrote an eloquent book about his search for it.[1] Like solitude in the Spanish concept of *soledad*, silence resembles a listening companion rather than a place emptied of all sounds. It has the attentive quality of a person. What is unspoken may be intended and therefore imply meaning. To this potential meaning within the silence, the Polish poet Cyprian Norwid (1821–83) would frequently return in his comments on literature, until he formulated them towards the end of his life in a study wholly devoted to Silence (*Milczenie*, 1882).

The focal point in his reasoning, both here and earlier, seems to be the significance of gaps whether between the lines of text or the lines of figurative art. They should not be overlooked, still less should they be ignored as mere vacuum. In a letter of November 1867, Norwid says this about formal perfection:

Perfect lyric poetry should be like a cast in plaster: the slashes where form passes form, leaving crevices, must be preserved and not smoothed out with the knife. Only the barbarian takes all this off from the plaster with his knife and destroys the whole.[2]

In speech, too, there are similar crevices, and if the grammarian smooths them out for the sake of his system, he destroys the function of silence. For Norwid silence is, in fact, a part of speech and he takes grammarians to task for refusing to recognize it as such. And yet, he says in his treatise, they are prepared to include exclamation among the parts of speech, although there is hardly any syntactic justification for this. You may find

---

[1] *Seven Storey Mountain*, published in England as *Elected Silence* (London, 1949). The second title alludes to G. M. Hopkins's early poem 'The Habit of Perfection' ('Elected Silence, sing to me').

[2] To Bronisław Zaleski. Norwid had a practical knowledge of art, he sculpted and painted. A number of his drawings have survived.

some semi-psychological reasons, but what does exclamation achieve? It breaks off a sequence of speech, slamming it like a door, whereas silences flow into an undercurrent and preserve a continuity.

Norwid used the term *przemilczenie* (i.e. something passed over in silence) to denote this structural function of silence. It can be discerned in every sequence, it links up sentences with one another. 'What the second sentence announces was in the previous sentence unsaid, that is, passed over in silence, what the third sentence says is rooted in the silence of the second',[1] and so on.

If we understand Norwid correctly, he seems to suggest that we use, quite naturally, a double conveyance of meaning: the silent and the audible, both dependent on each other, with silence preparing the voice for passage from phrase to phrase. One could almost imagine a sense of hearing so subtle that it would be able to understand the silent intermezzi by themselves, without the voice. Expressions like 'thinking aloud' or 'reading between the lines' are apt in what they infer; one could by analogy speak of 'following the thread of silence', or being 'rhetorically silent'.[2]

Norwid not only defines silence as a part of speech, but also sees its presence in every literary *genre*. And he can vouch for it himself. His lyrical poem 'The Ripe Laurel' describes silence as a gathering of voices,[3] his prose piece 'The White Flowers' has a remark about the 'horrifying chords of silence'.[4] He regards one of his early plays, *Zwolon*, as a 'many-voiced monologue'.[5] To this complex nature of the monologue he returns in the discourse *Milczenie* from which I have already quoted. Here he links it with his central notion of *przemilczenie*:

Speech, because it is speech, must be indispensably dramatic. Even the monologue is a conversation with oneself or with the spirit of the thing in question. It is almost impossible to think up a sentence so abstractedly pallid that it would bring no silence (*przemilczenie*) with itself.

---

[1] *Milczenie*, II. This part, containing the main arguments, is called 'grammatical, philosophical and exegetic'.

[2] These colloquial examples are mine, not Norwid's.

[3] '*Cisza jest głosów zbieraniem*', '*Laur dojrzały*' from the collection *Vade-mecum*.

[4] '*Cisz akordy straszne*', '*Białe kwiaty*'.

[5] Cf. '*Różnogłosego monologu/Na żadnej jeszcze scenie nie widziano*' ('*Wstęp*'). *Zwolon* (1851) is about anonymous, i.e. silent heroism.

Later he speaks of the attainable harmony between the outer and the inner ear and between the 'optical looking at' and *seeing*. All the sensory faculties in man strive after this deeper attainment. Norwid shows how man needs to rebuild his whole sensory perception which may be achieved through 'the long calm of silent stillness'.[1]

Some sixty years after Norwid, Eliot was to invoke the dark out of the stillness: 'I said to my soul be still, and let the dark come upon you'.[2] Norwid, too, knows about the mediatory nature of silence, beyond which lies the dark, and beyond the dark—the other side of silence. One has to forget grand juxta-positions, like that of Carlyle: 'Speech is of Time, Silence is of Eternity'.[3] We are close to the spiritual notions of St. John of the Cross, his dark night of the soul, and the *via negationis*.

Norwid, of course, was not a mystic in the contemplative sense. Few poets are. But he spoke with an authority of a high order which came, I think, from the recurring experience of *przemilczenie* in his own life. At the end of it he could look back and see himself being passed over in silence. The continuity of his work, so important to him, was broken by gaps: some of his manuscripts were lost, many had to wait for posthumous recog-nition in this century, and the few of his books that appeared in print between 1850 and 1870 met with almost no reaction.[4] Yet he tried to link them up, to give them a context filled with his comments, footnotes, and epigraphs; he wrote explanatory letters to those who he thought would care, piecing together a passionate apologia for his type of art.[5] His correspondence again was destined to be printed with gaps, for only a portion of it has survived. Crevices of meaningful silence remain for us to see.

Today Norwid's *Vade-mecum* stands as a monument to his preoccupation with speech and silence. It was planned to be a guide for future poetry; originally it had a hundred example-poems, carved from the knowledge of poetic diction, often apophthegmatic in character, but the *vade-mecum* intention was

---

[1] '*długim spokojem milczącej ciszy*'. Norwid distinguishes here between *spokój* (calm) and *cisza* (stillness) to avoid a verbal paradox. *Milczącej* means 'keeping silence'.

[2] *East Coker*, III.   [3] *Sartor Resartus*, Book III, chapter 3.

[4] Brockhaus published *Poezye Cypriana Norwida* (Leipzig, 1863), but declined to take *Vade-mecum*.

[5] For further examples in English, see Norwid's 'Letters and Poems' in *Botteghe Oscure* XXII (Autumn 1958).

frustrated by the fact that no reader, however willing, could accompany Norwid: the whole volume, though completed by 1865, had to remain an experiment on paper, exposed to physical damage and the risk of annihilation until it finally appeared in print after the last war, in 1947.[1] Whenever the poet opened the unlucky manuscript to make further revisions, he must have read the syllables of silence in each line, the meaning of his whole book delayed by neglect, removed from participation by others and left at the mercy of chance.

This was his own moral lesson drawn from the subtle acknow-ledgement of silence which could gather voices over the long decades at her discretion but at the expense of his fame. He said bitter things about the obscurity of which he was accused, about the irony which would be his only mourner,[2] and about the haste with which in the era of 'Print-Pantheism' he was being passed over, if read at all, an exegetist of Silence sacrificed to the dark goddess of Oblivion.

> I write—well, sometimes—to *Jerusalem*
> *Via Babylon*, and my letters arrive.
> It matters little if my views are then
> Proved right or wrong. An artist's memoirs thrive
> Through scribbles that turn inwards, loose again
> To something messy, crazy! But alive.[3]

2

In a historical sense Norwid's concept of *przemilczenie* works: there is a syntax within time: each age hands down to the next the latent voice of that which it kept unsaid or could not say. Once the past silence becomes audible, its meaning is already linked to the unsaid sequence of tomorrow. This can be com-pared to the process of realized meanings within the human psyche, the dark silence of the unconscious developing towards its future expression which, in fact, is already moulded. Jung had a wise answer when asked what we should do to avoid

---

[1] In a photographic reproduction of the original manuscript. The printed edition of 10,000 copies came out as late as 1964.

[2] '*A któż zapłacze po nas—kto? oprócz Ironii*', '*Do Walentego Pomiana Ż.*', epilogue to *Vade-mecum*.

[3] 'The people's hands were swollen with applause' ('*Klaskaniem mając obrzękłe prawice*'), from *Vade-mecum*, translated by Christine Brooke-Rose and J. Peter-kiewicz, *Botteghe Oscure*, op. cit.

future evil. 'We are the origin of all coming evil.' In other words, we have already sown the seeds of future evil, 'the only real danger that exists is man himself'.[1]

In a historical sense Norwid has to some extent received his due: much of his supposed obscurity has yielded meaning after the passing of *his* time sequence into *ours*. The benevolent nineteenth-century idols of progress and mass propaganda, the righteous makers of ideology, have turned into twentieth-century monsters whose presence he sensed and tried to exorcise through his poetry. He was not a romantic visionary, he reacted with his intellect and irony against the romantic prognostications:[2] time, past and present, was for him, like the silent links in human communication, an interlocking continuum. What is by-passed in the continuum of the present will be retraced in a future sequence: for the future is, as Norwid calls it, 'the eternal corrector', *korektorka-wieczna*.[3] We may be delivering a monologue out of despair, with no listener in sight, but silence will absorb it and change it into a dialogue at some point in the continuum of the future. In this lies hope. For the obscure gaps, whether in life or in art, need not be as frightening as a precipice. The drama of existence is not all voice. Nor is it voice heard only at a given time. It has its silences, pauses, and gestures in lieu of words.

> And whether the lip speak, or in inspired
> Silence, we clasp our hearts as a shut book
> Of song unsung, the silence and the speech
> Is each his [God's].[4]

[1] Interview with John Freeman on the B.B.C. television programme 'Face to Face', October 1959.

[2] 'We—the pale émigré faces—like those of the Nazarenes who know what will be in a thousand years, but what they have under their very hands is to them spellbound and unapproachable' (from a letter to B. Zaleski, December 1857).

[3] '*Do Walentego Pomiana Z.*'

[4] These lines come from P. J. Bailey's *Festus* (London, 1839), a dramatic poem now forgotten but once widely read. Bailey was no Norwid, yet he expressed a thought similar to his. *Festus* ran into many editions, and was revised. It is unfortunately very long and repetitive, though it contains striking lines. So does *The Mystic* (London, 1855), in which Bailey is capable of writing such phrases as: 'The myth-insculptured language of the light', and alliterative sequences like:

> One God omnific, sole, original
> Wise wonder-working wielder of the whole
> Infinite, inconceivable, immense . . .

Hopkins must have read this.

F

It is remarkable how much of Norwid's intuitive argument applies to the theatre of the unsaid which began perhaps earlier than in the plays of Samuel Beckett and Ionesco. We find the silent links in Strindberg who died in 1912 as well as in Maeterlinck who died in 1949, though the latter still waits for a sympathetic reappraisal. In Beckett's most successful play, *Waiting for Godot*, silences are an undercurrent of every dramatic situation, but they become a pattern of gaps almost visible to the audience when the messenger from Godot arrives for the second time. The pattern is intensified by the repeated 'Yes, sir' and 'No, sir', each new repetition being a reassuring echo and a meaning poised uncomfortably on the silence which may contain either the truth or the threat. The author is precise in his indications. I quote a part of this sequence:

Vladimir: But he'll come tomorrow.
Boy: Yes, sir.
Vladimir: Without fail.
Boy: Yes, sir.
   Silence.
Vladimir: Did you meet anyone?
Boy: No, sir.
Vladimir: Two other . . . (*he hesitates*) . . . men?
Boy: I didn't see anyone, sir.
   Silence.
Vladimir: What does he do, Mr. Godot? (*Silence*) Do you hear me?
Boy: Yes, sir.
Vladimir: Well?
Boy: He does nothing, sir.
   Silence.[1]

The visible gaps inside the meaning remind one again of the crevices in Norwid's analogy between lyric poetry and sculpture. As for sculpture, we now have a further proof of how right the poet's intuition was a hundred years ago. Henry Moore has made the open gap serve the shape and also the texture of his works. The holes in his reclining figures partake of the meaning and the light which interprets it for the eye. They certainly do not weaken the solidity of the stone, as the holes gaping in the speech do not cause the dramatic strength to crumble.

What is, however, the next step to be taken by the artist

[1] *Waiting for Godot* (London, 1956), Act II.

aware of such possibilities within form? Samuel Beckett has pursued a ruthless logic of his own, and one of the results is the mime miniature, like *Act Without Words*, no longer the theatre of the unsaid but the speechless drama without the mediacy of dialogue or monologue.[1]

3

It would appear that the lyrical poet has even fewer steps to make if he wishes to reach the end of a blind alley. Some of his traditional forms are exercises in brevity, from the epitaph and the apophthegm to the sonnet and the song, both often used in lyrical cycles. Norwid wanted his unpublished *Vade-mecum* to show, through a collection of lyrical experiments, how form constantly passes form, producing decisive cuts, crevices, and shapes not unlike those in sculpture. In terms of poetic diction he revived the gnomic type of verse.[2] Conciseness is, in fact, what strikes one in most of his poems, a deliberate clipping of voice, almost to the point of oracular utterance.

There remains, of course, a final challenge which comes not from the silence enclosed within human speech but from that other Silence which for the religious poet can only signify a link with the Word. And the Word was with God, says the apostle John. A young poet echoes it in a hieratic apostrophe:

> In the beginning was the word, the word
> That from the solid bases of the light
> Abstracted all the letters of the void.[3]

Those who claim to have listened hard *towards* that other reality, believe that God speaks to them through silences. But the poet who grapples with silence in the very mould of his words, knows that such a final challenge or temptation may simply mean the death of poetry. Would its death be more acceptable to him under the name of sacrifice? This, too, has to be answered.

[1] A parallel process seems to have affected his novels, if we take *Imagination Dead Imagine* (1965) to be a novel. Its brevity, seven pages in all, a mere thousand words, suggests a stylistic joke.

[2] I have dealt with the problem elsewhere, in 'Cyprian Norwid's *Vade-mecum*: An Experiment in Didactic Verse', *The Slavonic Review* (January 1966).

[3] Dylan Thomas, 'In the beginning was the three-pointed star', *18 Poems*.

CHAPTER VIII

SACRIFICE

I

Norwid refused to be bullied by battle cries and suicidal appeals. If this was anti-romantic for a man of his generation, it was also a proof of intellectual courage. He had to grow up in Warsaw after the November rising of 1830, and later as a voluntary exile he had to experience the shock of another insurrection in 1863. Between these two national blood sacrifices he published his 'many-voiced monologue' in which we read:

> They all hurry to death.
> And is there anyone who can look for life?
> How eager they all are to die for liberty,
> As if the cemetery alone could be called free.[1]

Yet in 1852, a year after the publication of these sane words, Norwid was on the run himself. He decided, quite suddenly, to leave Europe for the United States. A number of reasons contributed to this: an unhappy love for a rich, spoilt woman, who had called him a 'gamin' and treated him accordingly, his own financial insecurity, need of change, and a destructive urge which accompanied his artistic pride. Out of pride and frustration he wanted a fire sacrifice for his literary works. 'Burn all the manuscripts I sent you,' he wrote on departure to his friend Bohdan Zaleski.[2] The same desperate request went to a woman who had been a sympathetic confidante: 'Please burn all that bears my name. Let the world forget him who cannot come to any understanding with it.'[3]

This was undoubtedly meant. There had to be a sacrifice if the dramatic change, brought about by his own action, was to be a sincere start to his *vita nuova* which America, a new world, symbolized geographically. While in America, Norwid tried his

---

[1] From the play *Zwolon*. The title is an etymological coinage from *wola* (will), i.e. Norwid's hero is attuned to the will of God.

[2] Letter of 1852 (no date).

[3] Letter to Konstancja Górska, November 1852.

best to alter his precarious circumstances: now drawing and illustrating became for a time his source of income. He certainly wanted to be practical. But his new life in the geographical sense soon came to an end: in 1854 he returned to Europe.

The *vita nuova* of the spirit, however, continued; the intended sacrifice had not been in vain. Norwid still wrote, and much. He sent his manuscripts to publishers and friends. Many of them were lost in the process. No publisher could be found in 1866 or later for Norwid's most ambitious collection of lyrical poems, *Vade-mecum*. This many-voiced experiment had to remain an offering to the future. He entered into a sacrificial relationship with his contemporaries. I call it sacrificial because to him an individual had to be first attuned to the will of God before he could make sense in society. And society, without knowing it, needed such a man for its own renewal, although ignoring his actual presence. In a sacrificial relationship, no individual, however unsuccessful in society, can be called a social misfit.

There is a unique parallel between Norwid and G. M. Hopkins that can be illustrated with examples not only from the lives and works of the two poets, but also from their respective posthumous revivals. In their poetic diction they exhibit similar features which in Norwid's case have to be traced to models outside the Polish tradition.[1] Stylistic analogies, however, are less important for this chapter. What matters is the sacrificial character of Hopkins's devotion to poetry, in both a personal and a religious sense. Like Norwid in 1852, Hopkins in 1868 decided to make an end to his poetic vocation before entering a religious order. He told Richard Watson Dixon in a letter dated 5 October 1878: 'What I had written I burnt before I became a Jesuit and resolved to write no more, as not belonging to my profession unless it were the wish of my superiors.' More or less the same information is given in a letter of 29 October 1881:

I destroyed the verse I had written when I entered the Society and meant to write no more; the *Deutschland* I began after a long interval at the chance suggestion of my superior. . . . A very spiritual man

---

[1] For example, compounds of the kenning type, alliteration. I have discussed these and other stylistic parallels with Hopkins in an essay 'Introducing Norwid', *The Slavonic and East European Review* (December 1948).

once told me that with things like composition the best sacrifice was not to destroy one's work but to leave it entirely to be disposed of by obedience.

The mention of superiors is in keeping with the vow of obedience. Fame, it would seem, had little relevance to his situation, but he was not against having his poems published. 'The life I lead,' he wrote to Watson Dixon, 'is liable to many mortifications but the want of fame as a poet is the least of them. I could wish, I allow, that my pieces could at some time become known but in some spontaneous way, so to speak, and without my forcing' (12 May 1879).[1] It could be argued, of course, that one of the many mortifications had something to do with the curtailment of the imaginative faculty. Yet Hopkins was undoubtedly sincere in accepting the initial sacrifice.

Later he took pains to explain the peculiarities of his verse, such as sprung rhythm or idiosyncratic compounds, and his correspondence with Robert Bridges is particularly revealing in its examples of literary perfectionism. Added to the ideal of spiritual perfection, this must have intensified the tension within him. Moreover, the tension could not be resolved as long as his poetry remained an integral part of his spiritual exercises. For the poetry he wanted to write was also a discipline as strong as the religious. Both were essentially of a sacrificial kind, the vow of obedience and the ultimate denial of poetry, the second being further emphasized by the first. Their extreme manifestation seems to have led to a perfectionist's despair, permissible in art, but out of place in a religious vocation.

> I am gall, I am heartburn. God's most deep decree
> Bitter would have me taste: my taste was me;
> Bones built in me, flesh filled, blood brimmed the curse.
>   Selfyeast of spirit a dull dough sours. I see
> The lost are like this, and their scourge to be
> As I am mine, their sweating selves; but worse.[2]

Hopkins knew, from beginning to end, that there could be no choice for him, no alternative to the once accepted condition of being ready to give up his poetry, should a higher spiritual

---

[1] All three quotations come from *The Correspondence of Gerard Manley Hopkins and Richard Watson Dixon*, edited by C. C. Abbott (London, 1935).

[2] From the sonnet beginning 'I wake and feel the fell of dark, not day'.

necessity make this demand. He wrote, it seems, under a suspended sentence, which perhaps accounts for the strange feeling of limitation in his art, coming not from any formal deficiency but directly from the man himself. This, however, is also the poetic paradox of his greatness.

2

In contrast to Hopkins, Rimbaud had violent remedies for his inner tension and used them to the full. The publication of *Une Saison en Enfer* in 1873 brought him no fame, only rebuffs and indifference. The literary metropolis did not accept a genius from the provinces. So he walked back home, from Paris to Charleville, his pride broken, his disgust with authorship turning against his own work. He returned to punish himself in the place of his origin.

There is a story, confirmed by his younger sister, that he burnt his manuscripts and papers, and the copies of his book which he still had with him. This was a sacrifice in a visible sense, a physical act of destruction as well as a gesture towards spiritual renewal. Above all, it conforms to the character of Rimbaud, even though the authenticity of the event may never be fully proved. Analogous cases help us to understand the sacrificial motive.

Mickiewicz, for instance, burnt his papers and unfinished poems before going on his mission to Turkey. On 10 September 1855, his son Władysław witnessed this holocaust which preceded the poet's physical death by only a few months. It was not an offering of talent, but merely a handful of ashes cast over the unproductive period of twenty years.

Unlike Mickiewicz, Rimbaud had still eighteen years to live, a slow progress of annihilation. The poet was to be no more, only the man who had his body and bore his name. Whether or not Rimbaud wrote anything after *Une Saison en Enfer* is of little relevance to the final image which he himself left violently severed from his poetic identity. But could literary failure, however deeply disappointing, enforce such a complete denial of poetry? Rimbaud's sacrifice is, in fact, so unparalleled in the form it took and continued to take during his life of action in Africa, that one must regard it as a prolonged offering of the self. In a symbolic context, Rimbaud's example shows how immense the void becomes once the whole of poetry is expiated for.

Poetry was wrong, he apparently told his sister as he lay dying, he had given it up for this reason. Otherwise he would have plunged into madness with his dark magic. A visit to hell's sly hallucinations, '*une saison en enfer*', would have ended in a permanent confinement to evil. If he believed this to be a satisfactory explanation, he credited his will in the past with much power. 'But perhaps his renunciation,' Enid Starkie observes, 'was not entirely voluntary. . . . Perhaps he could no longer write when he ceased to believe that he saw God face to face.'[1] The void opened and he entered it to prove himself capable of living without magic. When he died, the sacrificial relationship passed on to his posthumous fame and created a magnetic power, attracting people to his verse. The sacrifice, it seems, had been offered to the future.

Rimbaud set an impossible example. No poet after him could emulate the sacrificial relationship to that extent and with as much simplicity. In modern times the situation has been almost reversed. Neither black nor white magic is taken at its original value. And since hallucinations are now chemically produced, they are thought to be controllable. Facts appear and vanish at a greater speed. History, too, has recently shown an unpleasant readiness to catch up with us before we can give visionaries a chance. If the need of sacrifice is still with the artist, the need should be minimized by rational motives to put his mind at rest. Is sacrifice worth much or is it even good enough for our age? It is repeatedly suggested to the poets that they should not attack big questions, for their vision may be easily invalidated by events of unprecedented magnitude like the Hiroshima holocaust.[2]

According to Donald Davie, for example, history caught up with Ezra Pound and 'passed him even as he wrote his poem'. This is how Davie argues before reaching his conclusion:

[1] *Arthur Rimbaud* (London, 1947), Part II, chapter X.
[2] '. . . It has been impossible since the outbreak of the second World War, and certainly from the time of Hiroshima, for any poet living near the centre of the crisis to make secular pronouncements concerning the world and its fate, or concerning man's place in the Universe. Events have dwarfed all possible comment.' J. M. Cohen, *Poetry of This Age, 1908–1958* (London, 1960), chapter X.

But the poet's vision of the centuries of recorded time has been invalidated by the *Cantos* in a way that invalidates also much writing by Pound's contemporaries. History, from now on, may be transcended in poetry, or it may be evaded there; but poetry is not the place where it may be understood.[1]

Ezra Pound has already written his sacrificial lines in the *Pisan Cantos*. I refer, of course, to the passage beginning with 'Pull down thy vanity'. Will the *Cantos* remain unfinished because they are monumental, just like those poem-ruins left by the romantic seers? What else is there to sacrifice for the poet who suffered humiliation and confinement to an asylum? It is often reported that now, in his old age, Pound refuses to pronounce any opinions. In fact, he declines to speak. I think that this is a sacrificial withdrawal, or, to put it differently, a sacrifice of that part of the self which knew well how to communicate with rebels, pundits, and the innocent. Pound the promoter of other people's careers, adviser and mentor to the young, has closed himself in, shutting off the words which he once used to send on errands:

> Go, my songs, to the lonely and the unsatisfied,
> Go also to the nerve-racked, go to the enslaved-by-convention,
> Bear to them my contempt for their oppressors.[2]

The question is: does he still believe in his poetry? Only he can answer this. In a moving interview given to an Italian journalist he says: 'This is it: all my life I believed I knew something. Then came a strange day, and I saw that I knew nothing. Yes, that I knew nothing. And words have become emptied of their meaning.' And again: 'I have lost the power of reaching the depth of my thought with words . . . I would like to explain: I . . . I . . . Ah, but everything is so difficult, everything is so useless.'[3]

Pasternak's success with *Dr. Zhivago* cannot be separated from the political sensation it aroused. The hysterics of both praise and abuse have already subsided. But what remains from the aura of the book illuminates the poet rather than the novelist. Pasternak, too, made an offering which he placed like

[1] *Ezra Pound, Poet as Sculptor* (London, 1965), chapter XIII.

[2] 'Commission', from *Lustra*.

[3] Interview with Grazia Livi in *Epoca* (Milan), 24 March 1963 (author's translation).

a wreath on his reputation. *Dr. Zhivago* begins with a funeral; this sets the tone, but the novel as a whole is a burial ground of poetry. He himself tried to justify his new faith in prose. In a conversation with Olga Carlisle, Pasternak said:

> I believe that it is no longer possible for lyric poetry to express the immensity of our experience. Life has grown too cumbersome, too complicated. We have acquired values which are best expressed in prose. I have tried to express them through my novel.[1]

He was, of course, making a point about lyrical verse, and this allowed for a clear-cut contrast with the narrative form. In fictional disguise Zhivago's profession is medicine, but he stands for the poetic I, and writing verses is a spiritual cure for him. *Medice, cura te ipsum*. The poet-novelist even within his only novel falls back on lyrical expression. This is significant in view of Pasternak's later pronouncement on its limitations. How sure was he, in fact, about sacrificing poetry for prose? Why should his Zhivago seek our sympathy through a lyrical medium?

One has to make the usual allowances for an impromptu statement in an interview, nevertheless Pasternak appears to be convincing himself. And his preference for prose is not only conditioned by the complexities of the twentieth century, if we recall that Rimbaud too discovered virtue in functional prose when he was on the verge of disowning poetry. The difference, however, lies in our readiness to accept Pasternak's opinion rather than Rimbaud's. We think we understand Rimbaud's adolescent anger. Pasternak belongs to our self-conscious age which has, after all, succeeded in diminishing the status of the poet. 'The poet may one day be honoured again as a seer',[2] a modern critic, Donald Davie, writes, knowing perfectly well that any bardic gesture would be unacceptable today.

The poet has stepped down from the pedestal. This is to his credit, or so we think, preferring to see a poet in an ordinary profession, a bank clerk, a librarian, a publisher. This may be a good way of paying sacrificial dues to society. But the sacrificial relationship in the past had a fuller impact. A perfectionist's despair like that of Hopkins demanded total risks in form. There

[1] 'Three Visits with Boris Pasternak' in *The Paris Review* No 24 (Summer-Fall, 1960).

[2] *Ezra Pound, Poet as Sculptor*, op. cit., chapter **XIII**.

was no compromise in the sacrificial dedication of Norwid, Hopkins, or Rimbaud, though it could lead to catastrophe. Perhaps the symbol of the altar cannot be removed altogether from the concept of sacrifice.

3

Pasternak contrasted the novel with lyrical verse. The epic poem did not enter into his comparison as a form impossible to revive in the present age. Virgil left us no record of his thoughts about the *Aeneid*. But tradition has handed down the story that he was profoundly dissatisfied and wanted to burn his poem. Had he succeeded, it would have been a major offering on the sacrificial altar of literature. Emperor Augustus intervened and Virgil's wish was overruled by authority.

There are, no doubt, many different ways of imagining this sacrificial relationship between Virgil and posterity. Hermann Broch, I think, convincingly recreated the mood of the situation in his novel *The Death of Virgil*. Slowly he builds up the tension. The Emperor is shown as a friend, a tempter, an agent of fate and an abstract power. At one point in this verbal duel Virgil speaks of redemption which 'will come through the sacrifice'. But he is arguing with a man of action: 'Since I could not consecrate my whole life to sacrifice, as you have done yours, I must designate my work for this purpose. . . . It must sink out of memory, and I with it.'[1]

Finally, Augustus wins and Virgil sees the manuscript-chest being carried away. The last part of the book becomes rhapsodic in style. The poet hears the waves of sounds, his dying consciousness feels the presence of the word:

the universe disappearing before the word, dissolved and acquitted in the word while still being contained and preserved in it, destroyed and recreated forever, because nothing had been lost, nothing would be lost . . .

And later:

. . . the more unattainable, the greater, the graver and more elusive became the word, a floating sea, a floating fire, sea-heavy, sea-light, notwithstanding it was still the word: he could not hold

[1] *The Death of Virgil*, translated by Jean Starr Untermeyer (London, 1946), Part III.

fast to it and he might not hold fast to it; incomprehensible and unutterable for him: it was the word beyond speech.[1]

One has to ask whether true sacrifice can be accomplished out of dissatisfaction or failure. Perhaps, on the contrary, it should come from the sense of achievement and recognition. A Polish critic, Karol Irzykowski, knew which was true when he wrote this epigram: 'The offering to the Muses: when everybody's verdict is good, the poet burns his work to pass the trial of fire.'[2]

The sacrificial relationship seems to express itself best in the symbol of fire which consumes while it illuminates.

[1] These are the final lines of Broch's novel.

[2] *Notatki z życia obserwacje i motywy* (Warsaw, 1964). The epigram appears in Irzykowski's notebook of 1891.

CHAPTER IX

THE PROPHET'S LEAP

I

At Cuma near Naples one enters the caves as a tourist, but soon the curiosity is changed into respect and reverence. One becomes a pilgrim, standing on sibyl's ground which has retained the authority of a sacred place. There, through the openings in the caves, humble voices asked for prophecy, and here under the vaulted rocks the voice of the Cumaean sibyl would resound from shadow to shadow.

It is impossible to disregard the strange fascination this place holds for us today. But why should it be so? Is this due to the mystery of inspiration which we still associate with poetry, or is it because of our interest in parapsychic phenomena? Virgil made his hero visit Cumae in the sixth book of the *Aeneid*. He himself was to be revered by Christians as a divinely inspired poet who in the Fourth Eclogue prophesied the coming of a Wonder-child from heaven, the firstborn of the new era: *iam nova progenies caelo demittitur alto.*

The eclogue is a good puzzling text for speculations, and many have been put forward over the centuries. But it hardly matters whether by his oracle Virgil meant a future child of Octavian or Antony or anybody else. He certainly set a trap for scholars.[1] What is of historical importance to poetry concerns Virgil's status as a prophet which his Christian readers, and especially writers like Dante, helped to raise high. In Virgil they found a classic example of divine inspiration; this enhanced the poet's place in society and invested his art with transcendental meaning.

For those therefore who considered poetry to be a potential

[1] E. V. Rieu has lucidly summarized the diverse problems: 'The Fourth Eclogue is a lyrical rhapsody. It is a Roman oracle, too. It is also a vision, conditioned by its date, but influenced none the less by those mysterious forces which, even as Virgil wrote, were gathering strength in Palestine to shape the future of mankind.' His essay is in Virgil, *The Pastoral Poems*, translated by E. V. Rieu (Penguin Classics, 1954).

vehicle of prophecy, the oracular content came first, before any form of verse which merely served as embellishment and at best as a veil. The poet had to be a seer rather than a maker. 'Hear the voice of the Bard! Who present, past and future sees'— this is how Blake introduced his *Songs of Experience*.

But something more was required from the inspired seer: he had to leap into the dark after his oracles. There was no winding way to the truth, only two distant points on a line of vision, and a jump. A seventeenth-century mystic from Silesia, Angelus Silesius, wrote about *ein Stüpfchen* (dot) and *ein Kreis* (circle) in *The Cherubic Wanderer*, suspending his epigrams over a precipice:

> Ich weiss nicht/was ich bin/ich bin nicht/ was ich weiss:
> Ein Ding und nicht ein Ding/ein Stüpfchen und ein Kreis.

> Ich bin so gross als Gott/er ist als ich so klein:
> Er kann nicht über mich/ich unter ihn nicht sein.[1]

The prophetic leap appealed to the Romantics who always hurried after their muse. Pushkin and Mickiewicz were brought up in the classicist tradition, yet it was the concept of the poet-seer that liberated them from eighteenth-century scepticism and modish irony to which they were both attracted. There had to be, however, some violent spiritual intervention before this liberation could be achieved. Pushkin in his poem 'The Prophet' (*Prorok*) makes this very clear. He begins with the familiar symbols of the desert and the crossroads and then paraphrases a passage from the Book of Isaiah, chapter 6 (the six-winged seraphim, the placing of a live coal from the altar on the prophet's mouth). The seraph opens the eyes and the ears of the poet, but he also tears out his tongue and his heart, replacing the heart with a coal of live fire.[2] Thus the body is submitted to the angel's purifying violence before it can receive a voice from God.

---

[1] I know not what I am, and what I know am not:
A thing and not a thing, a circle and a dot.

I am as large as God, and He as small as I;
I cannot lower be; He cannot be more high.
The English version is that of Frank J. Warnke in his *European Metaphysical Poetry* (New Haven, 1961).

[2] Yeats uses the same theme in the lines:
Soul: Ezekiel's coal and speech leaps out anew.
Heart: Can there be living speech in heaven's blue?
(Quoted in the letter to Olivia Shakespear of 3 January 1932.)

It is not surprising that Mickiewicz, who had met Pushkin in Russia, saw in 'The Prophet' the true poetic credentials which he could not find in Pushkin's other works. Mickiewicz himself measured his own achievement against this prophetic ideal. When he stopped writing verse, the oracular urge remained and soon came to the surface. It distorted the purpose of his lectures on Slavonic literatures, which he began at the Collège de France in December 1840.[1] In the final stage, all academic pretence gone, he preached his Messianic gospel and invoked the holy name of Napoleon. Irony would have it that only ten years after the French government had relieved him of his post, Mickiewicz could extol Napoleon III at war in a Latin ode. By then he had been given employment at the Bibliothèque de l'Arsenal. His last leap into the dark came during the Crimean War in 1855, the year of his death.

I have used the example of Mickiewicz in different contexts, for each of them seems to confirm his profound dissatisfaction with poetry. The lectures he delivered at the Collège de France may be an embarrassment to scholarship, but they are certainly self-revealing, especially in the strict interpretation of poetry which at its highest must be visionary. In support he quotes Louis-Claude de Saint-Martin, the eighteenth-century illuminist, whom he greatly admired: Art is and can be nothing else than the presentation of a vision (*'L'art n'est et ne peut être que la représentation d'une vision'*). Artists are people who have, often without knowing it, the gift of visions.[2] Future poetry, according to Mickiewicz, will be written by poets only when they experience divine inspiration. The ideal is 'to cast aside from Poetry all that is not Inspiration'—Mickiewicz would have applauded this line from Blake.[3] By reverting to the practice of the Hebrew prophets, the poet-seer will serve the true Orphic spirit. There is nothing else for him but the highest order; prophetic poetry is precisely this: *'La poésie du premier ordre'*. Saint-

[1] This sad episode in the poet's life is fully discussed by W. Weintraub in *Literature as Prophecy* (The Hague, 1959). On Mickiewicz and Pushkin, see W. Lednicki, 'Ex oriente lux', in *Semitic and Oriental Studies* (Berkeley, Calif.), vol. XI, 1951.

[2] *Sixième Leçon*, 30 January 1844. The text is in A. Mickiewicz, *Les Slaves* (Paris, 1914).

[3] From *Milton*, where Blake quotes a significant line from the Bible: 'Would to God that all the Lord's people were Prophets' (Numbers 11: 29).

Martin asserts, in fact, too much, when he identifies the function of art with the representation of visions.[1]

This emphasis on mediation and reproduction, despite all the mysticism, recalls the aesthetics of the eighteenth-century classicists; it is like the imitation of nature, based on the belief that there are forms of perfection for the artist to seek and recapture. Furthermore, reproducible visions have, it would seem, something in common with Plato's Forms: they too cast shadows on to our lower existence. In any metaphysical inference from aesthetics one invariably goes back to the early notions about the duality of spirit and matter, perennial antitheses and allegorical parallels. In the Middle Ages, for instance, the allegorical function of visions was exemplified in the dream-formula which we find in the *Roman de la Rose*, *Piers Ploughman*, Boccaccio's *Olympia*, Chaucer's *Book of the Duchess*, and even as late as in Kochanowski's cycle of laments (*Treny*, 1580). This framework could not be sustained for long, once the allegorical system of correspondences had lost its appeal, but the poets went on using the dream as a mediator of visions, however personal their cause might be.

2

> I had a dream, which was not all a dream,
> The bright sun was extinguish'd, and the stars
> Did wander darkling in the eternal space . . .

This is how Byron begins his vision, 'Darkness', in which he effectively describes the icy earth, the cities and forests set on fire, the famine, until the world becomes 'seasonless, herbless, treeless, manless, lifeless'. The poem is an attempt to see through the dark glass into the future.

Mickiewicz responded to Byron's gloomy oracle and translated it into Polish.[2] Dream and vision have special significance among his own lyrics: they are treated as prophetic records. The poem 'I dreamt of winter' (*Śniła się zima*) is preceded by a note which gives the full date of a dream he had in Dresden,[3]

---

[1] Both early and recent studies on Saint-Martin come, understandably enough, from apologists, such as M. Matter, *Saint Martin, Le philosophe inconnu* (Paris, 1862), and R. Christoflour, *Prophètes du XIXe Siècle* (Paris, 1954).   [2] '*Ciemność*'.

[3] In Dresden, too, he wrote Part III of his drama *Dziady*, where he frequently shows the nature of good and evil in a vision or a dream, e.g. the vision of Father Piotr (Scene 5) and the nightmarish dreams of the Russian Senator (Scene 6).

and a further note testifies that 'these lines were written down as they came, without reflection and corrections'. Another poem is simply called 'Vision' (*Widzenie*) and begins with a vivid description: 'A sound struck me—and like a field flower rounded off with down, my body burst, plucked by the angel's breeze.' Here again, as in Pushkin's poem about the prophet, the senses are overpowered by a spiritual event. Only then can the eyes partake of a vision. A psychological transformation has taken place.

Coleridge concocted a factual note to his 'Kubla Khan'. Misleading it may be, nevertheless it speaks of 'a psychological curiosity'. The poem came to him as 'a vision in a dream';[1] this is confirmed in the subtitle, but the process of writing it down was apparently interrupted by a visitor on business from Porlock. Hence the fragment instead of a complete work. Whether this is true or not, some significance is attached to the poem being a fragment. The Romantics wanted to see their visions in the way they saw ruins, broken up and abandoned. Then they imagined the whole, and tried to leap into the dark, at least with one of their senses. If this succeeded, the suddenness of illumination meant more than the vision itself and had to be reflected in words.

The more the poet adhered to his dream signs, the more he tried to rush through the rendering of them, so that in the end he worked at the speed of notes. This happened to Słowacki who jotted down his dreams as if he wanted to oblige some future psychoanalyst. In the Notebook (*Raptularz*), kept between 1843 and 1847, dream is treated as a means of spiritual communication with outer and inner reality, the latter being buried inside oneself. This leads to a pronouncement on poets who, according to Słowacki, 'are the great excavators of words prompted to them by spirits, and these words used in rhymes have a power of revelation'. Some of Słowacki's jottings suggest this power. 'A sacrifice from colours—for light in the future.' A cryptic line, yet it sounds meaningful like a message in a dream. Since poets are dream diviners and therefore in touch with the laws of the spirit, they could be called the legislators of the world; Shelley and Słowacki seem to think similar thoughts. But the oracular glimpses into the future, whether guided by dreams, fantasy, or

[1] Coleridge recounts dreams also in his Notebooks, e.g. 10 November 1803.

G

by intuition, brought Słowacki, during the 1840s, close to scientific speculations which were later recognized as a poet's groping for a theory of evolution.

Again and again, Słowacki grappled with the diverse forms in matter, 'the chain of forms', and saw in them the continuous work of genesis. His concept of genesis, however, was spiritual, *Genesis from the Spirit*, as the title of his prose tract on evolution proclaimed (1844), and the style of the tract was that of prayer. He writes imaginatively of extinct giant creatures, plant-reptiles, languid monsters: of their shapes which evolved the human form. 'In each shape,' Słowacki declares with oracular insight,

there is, as it were, the memory of the previous and the revelation of the next form, and in all the shapes together there is the revealing (*rewelatorstwo*) of mankind, the dreaming of forms as it were about man. Man was for a long time the final aim of the spirit creating on earth.

The whole of *Genesis from the Spirit* is illuminated by such passages, each giving proof of the prophetic leap into the dark. When Darwin's book *On the Origin of Species by Means of Natural Selection* (1859) caused dismay among the religious believers, a few apologists looked in vain for the spiritual missing link. At the turn of the century in Poland, Słowacki posthumously offered some consolation to those who wanted to reconcile science with religion. *Genesis from the Spirit* found admirers who exaggerated its importance, treating the poet almost as a forerunner of Darwin.[1] Today, oddly enough, that prophetic leap of Słowacki appears to have landed him further, next to the ideas which are now spanning the same gap between science and theology. And it is, as often happens in true analogies, a matter of style in comparable contexts.

Teilhard de Chardin at his oracular best uses the kind of language which the late Romantics were fond of.[2] The evolu-

[1] W. Lutosławski, *Darwin i Słowacki* (Warsaw, 1909).

[2] His rhapsodic tone is not lost in English translation:

A glow ripples outward from the first spark of conscious reflection. The point of ignition grows larger. The fire spreads in ever widening circles till finally the whole planet is covered with incandescence. Only one interpretation, only one name can be found worthy of this grand phenomenon. Much more coherent and just as extensive as any preceding layer, it is really a new layer, the 'thinking layer', which, since its germination at the end of the Tertiary period, has spread over and above the world of plants and animals.

The Phenomenon of Man, translated by Bernard Wall (London, 1959), III, chapter 1.

tion he describes is also viewed *sub specie aeternitatis*, with Christ
at 'point Omega', in whom all things are epitomized. Teilhard's
terminology, 'Nous-sphere' for example, has proved an obstacle
to some of his sympathetic critics. Occasionally, his manner of
presentation has to be oracular. And Słowacki, announcing to
the world the new Alpha and Omega, sounds at times as if he
were addressing the Teilhards of our age. This is how he intones his prayer towards the end of his tract: 'Let it be that
from this Alpha and from Christ and from your Word, the
whole world shall be evolved.' Whatever one thinks of the
reliability of intuitive statements, Słowacki presents a good
case for the defence of the sibylline heritage in poetry.

So does Rimbaud. The striking thing about Rimbaud's entry
into literature is that it looked exactly like a prophet's leap. All
of a sudden there he stood in the midst of language, not a
baffled apprentice, but one who from the start behaved like a
master, summoning the vocabulary of heaven and hell, order-
ing vowels to show him their true colours. Had Mickiewicz lived
sixteen years longer, he might have seen a proof of Saint-
Martin's dictum about art reproducing visions. At last a boy-
prophet had arisen, a perfect mediator who bore Apollo's
oracle inscribed on his forehead.[1] Enid Starkie in her excellent
study of Rimbaud[2] gives much information about his prophetic
heritage which is rooted in the occult sciences, the Cabala, and
the hermetic philosophy (alchemy). Martinez Pasqualis and his
pupil Saint-Martin come into the picture, linking in a fascinat-
ing way the Cabalistic interests of Mickiewicz with those of
Rimbaud.

What Saint-Martin expected from future poetry, Rimbaud
tried in fact to practise at the risk of being destroyed by his own
hermetic experiment. For a time he seemed to be holding the
philosopher's stone. Like another early nineteenth-century illuminist, Ballanche, he worked the old tricks of alchemy into
Christian dogma which, after all, was not easily transmutable.
To Ballanche the world represented God's thought written
down, but man, having lost his primordial faculty, could no

---

[1] As a schoolboy Rimbaud composed a Latin poem in which Apollo writes on
his brow with a flame, '*Tu vates eris*' (You'll be a seer). The Muses repeat this
prophecy.

[2] *Arthur Rimbaud*, op. cit.

longer read the script of nature. Only a new Orpheus, he hoped, would one day restore the connexion severed from the divine intelligence.

3

Obviously, ideas of this kind were welcomed by poets. And they were very much in the air after the beginning of the nineteenth-century. Herder and the Schlegels taught that poetry was the first expression of man. Blake, Wordsworth, Shelley, Novalis, Mickiewicz, Słowacki, and to a certain degree Coleridge, Push-kin, Lermontov, Espronceda, and Leopardi accepted the high mission of *vates*, the poet-seer. Threatened by the scientific know-how of their age, they felt more secure when their intuitive powers were still considered to be above all other sources of knowledge.

The future, according to Ballanche, was the present seen clearly.[1] This meant seeing higher rather than further. The poet's range of vision allowed him to glance over all the past generations and into the present-future. If someone like Bal-lanche could claim that for poets, a really bold practitioner of verse was bound to take it for granted. With superb self-confidence Walt Whitman wrote in his preface to *Leaves of Grass*:

> The greatest poet forms the consistence of what is to be, from what has been and is. He drags the dead out of their coffins and stands them again on their feet. He says to the past, Rise and walk before me that I may realize you. He learns the lesson—he places himself where the future becomes present.

This is certainly aggressive by comparison with Słowacki who merely wanted to excavate the words of the spirits. Even Shelley willingly submitted himself to the spirit manifested in the air, he did not shout orders at the west wind. With Whit-man each prophetic leap is that of an athlete. In *Song of My-self* he declared that he was the teacher of athletes; yes, he

---

[1] '*L'avenir, c'est le présent bien vu. Qu'étaient les prophètes? Leur nom dit ce qu'ils étaient. Ils s'appelaient les voyants.*' '*Elégie*' VII, in *Oeuvres* (Paris-Geneva, 1830), vol. I. It is worth recalling Blake's bard 'who present, past and future sees'.

Enid Starkie devotes a whole chapter to Pierre-Simon Ballanche (1776–1847) in her book on Rimbaud. The context is extendable: Ballanche, like Saint-Simon, owed much to Jacob Böhme, and his ideas of expiation and social palingenesis linked him with C. Bonnet, Herder, Vico.

was large, he contained multitudes. This makes Mickiewicz's Million sound almost modest, and he called himself that because he suffered for millions.[1] Perhaps the athletics of prophecy aim at banishing man's fear of the future, yet neither Saint-Martin nor Ballanche, one feels, would have approved of playing safe.

Rimbaud never played safe. Like Whitman, he could sound aggressive in a mood of mystical reverence, but unlike Whitman, he was vulnerable from the start, a boy prophet heading towards his own exile. When the time came, he chose Africa. Perhaps he obeyed his heart which sensed brothers in the unknown blacks.

> . . . Mon coeur, c'est sûr, ils sont des frères:
> Noirs inconnus, si nous allions! Allons! allons![2]

He found himself, it seems, at the end of his prophecy. Although aware that the old world of empires, colonies, and republics was to end as well, the poet-alchemist abandoned his search for instant gold and became an adventurer trader who had to accept gold at its prosaic value. For all he knew and cared, the age of Theophany might still be round the corner but the prophet in Rimbaud had left him worn out at the age of twenty.

At this point it is worth recalling what Yeats said in *The Wild Swans at Coole*: 'I am worn out with dreams.' He was then fifty-two. A theosophist, a myth-diviner, a lover of folklore, Yeats leapt from one occult venture to another, the poetic Theophany within reach yet like a dream difficult to retain.[3] In his celebrated lines, 'Surely some revelation is at hand,/Surely the Second Coming is at hand,' the repeated *surely* betrays the mood of uncertainty and *some* does not make the revelation all that certain.

Trying to look over God's shoulder into his secret designs turns out to be a new temptation, just as a shortcut to knowledge through magic is a mere temptation. Rimbaud regretted his dabbling in magical practices and believed he was cursed for this. Yet *Les Illuminations* remain illuminated by the shafts of

---

[1] *Dziady*, Part III, Scene 2.

[2] '*Qu'est-ce pour nous, mon coeur, que les nappes de sang*'.

[3] Cf. Wordsworth's 'Whither is fled the visionary gleam?/Where is it now, the glory and the dream?' (*Ode on the Intimations of Immortality*).

light coming from the doors of perception, to use Blake's phrase. These doors are never fully open, though a child's hand can keep them ajar, and Rimbaud trusted his hand.

If the doors of perception let in light, the sibylline caves release darkness, for they have no doors. There is a meaning in this contrast, applicable to the poet-seer whose revelations, no matter how valid they are, must be momentary. You leap into the dark or out of the dark. A light, however small, seems to release all darkness. That is why Blake, Saint-Martin, and Mickiewicz wanted to identify poetry with prophecy. Their message to poets is: if you can't leap after a speck of divine light, stand still; if you can't speak with an oracular voice, don't speak at all.

To any other practitioner of verse this amounts to the death of poetry. To a poet who, like Rimbaud, begins with vision, nothing else will do after the loss of it: in practice this also means the death of poetry.

'Could I revive within me'—a conditional marks in 'Kubla Khan' a sense of loss. Out of this a plain admission will come three years later, 'The Poet is dead in me.' Significantly, Coleridge ends his fragment of vision with a warning about the participant in that illumination: beware his flashing eyes, his floating hair, weave a circle round him thrice. This is a small spell of magic against unknown magic whose full release would flood the gates of perception.

A modern thinker, Martin Buber, phrases his warning differently. 'Magic,' he says in *I and Thou*, 'desires to obtain its effects without entering into relation, and practises its tricks in the void.'[1] Rimbaud recognized the dread of the void and withdrew. When Rilke turned to magic in his arid period, before writing *The Duino Elegies*, he was trying to enter into relation, and found that it could not be precipitated by dipping the mind in the occult.[2] He had to be patient and wait for the visitation of his angels.

In essence, then, Buber's dismissal of magic resembles Saint-Martin's rejection of any poetic artifice which takes the place of inspiration. All illuminists agree on this: you cannot conjure up

[1] *Ich und Du*, 1923, translated by R. G. Smith as *I and Thou* (Edinburgh, 1937)
[2] For examples of Rilke's interest in the occult see Marie von Thurn und Taxis-Hohenlohe, *Erinnerungen an Rainer Maria Rilke* (Munich-Berlin, 1933).

Theophany; to be inspired means to enter into relation. I and Thou need no mediator. The leaping prophet leaps in fact for joy that it should be so.

4

The joy is manifest in Blake's writing, and he had no fear of appearing ridiculous, a condition of mind necessary to an easily excitable prophet. But he seems to contradict both Saint-Martin's dictum and Rimbaud's practice. Under his pen prophecies multiply, the divine spring bubbles for him with Gnostic indiscretions about Heaven and Hell, and Blake reports the holy scandals in the language of *sancta simplicitas*.

> Grown old in love from seven till seven times seven,
> I oft have wish'd for Hell, for ease from Heaven.[1]

> Was Jesus chaste? or did He
> Give any lessons of chastity?[2]

The sheer length of his prophetic books, however, works against their content.[3] Here Blake's visionary participation is of the kind which forbids the reader's participation, and the *sancta simplicitas* of tone is absent. *The Book of Thel, America, Europe, The Book of Urizen, The Song of Los,* for all their volatile passages, deflate themselves in the end like prophetic balloons, and the mechanics of verse labour in the Ossianic fog. It is *fin-de-siècle* stuff, though eighteenth century.

What attracts us to Blake is his loathing of hypocrisy and his mystical polemics which cut through codified visions. As a child he was punished by his mother for having met Ezekiel under a green bough. One would like to be innocent enough to believe this story.

'If the doors of perception were cleansed everything would appear to man as it is, infinite.' Aldous Huxley took this memorable sentence from *The Marriage of Heaven and Hell* and used it as the title of his essay on the mescalin experience.[4] The choice was appropriate. But this short-cut to vision, achieved with the help of an old Mexican drug, was bound to incite the

---

[1] One of his gnomic verses.   [2] 'The Everlasting Gospel'.
[3] The same is true of the visionary writing of Victor Hugo, e.g. *La Fin de Satan*.
[4] *The Doors of Perception* (London, 1954).

curiosity of the public at large. Soon the scientific inquiry deteriorated into a gimmick and a social menace.

Vision is available for kicks, prophecy can now pass from a drugged mind to a tape recorder. For some LSD (lysergic acid diethylamide) has already opened the gates of hell and released horror in gory super-colour. Much more, no doubt, will gush or ooze from mental space and the void beyond it. Magic practising tricks in the void, as Buber said, with only I and no Thou.

Should we then create favourable clinical conditions for the poet-seer, supply him with drugs and expect to get in return oracles on tape, automatic reportage from the dark inside, backed with the sibyl's echoes? Such possibilities will be pursued, no doubt. For the time being, one could make a few lines from Hopkins serve as a motto, conveniently prophetic in its semantic nuances:

> ... O óur oracle. Lét life, wáned, ah lét life wind
> Off her once skéined stained véined varíety upon, áll on twó
> spools. ... [1]

Black, white, right, wrong; these two—and Hopkins ends with a rack, thoughts in groans grinding against thoughts. No leaping prophet, it seems, jumps over that obstacle, alive.

[1] 'Spelt from Sybil's Leaves'.

CHAPTER X

THE NIGHT JOURNEY

I

I have tried to describe different phenomena by which we can recognize the poet's crisis. Each of them is a manifestation of the death-wish which I regard as a permanent condition of poetry. The crisis then is in one sense unavoidable and in another impossible to predict because it can occur even at a youthful age, since most poets are early beginners. What, however, distinguishes the phenomena is the active presence of imagination. When it goes, nothing is clearly recognizable, and the dark night begins. While the poet is still working out his crisis through silence, sacrifice, prophetic sighting, or by clinging to some concrete and verifiable detail, his imagination is working with him. The senses may already be knocking against the limits of language, but this, after all, happens to our understanding in each daily encounter with words.[1] The dark night means the total blackout of imagination: the senses are numbed and the psychic journey is reduced to waiting.

At this point the poet most resembles the mystic; he has to be passive in order to find himself on the other side. Nothing will guide him there and he knows of nothing that could equal his absent imagination. Passively, he accepts that poetry as experience, tool, or purpose is of no further use. It has led him to this dark halt and the words, laid down in lines like a track, end abruptly in nowhere. The unimaginable is what surrounds him now in his state of waiting.

The mystical verse of St. John of the Cross reveals something of this state, but it also reveals gaps which belong to the indiscernible progress of the dark night. The same applies to the chronology of his poems which straddles crevasses of time in

---

[1] 'The results of philosophy are the uncovering of one or another piece of plain nonsense and of bumps that the understanding has got by running its head up against the limits of language. These bumps make us see the value of the discovery.' Ludwig Wittgenstein, *Philosophical Investigations*, translated by G. E. M. Anscombe (Oxford, 1953), para. 119.

contemplation. Writing, like contemplation, tends to be disrupted. Thus he wrote some of his verses during the eight months of his imprisonment at the Carmelite priory at Toledo (1577–8), the others were completed when he lived in Andalusia. Then came his four prose works on contemplation in which he interpreted three of his poems.[1] To a certain degree St. John's prose imposes a logical pattern on the chosen texts. Out of their spontaneity it develops a mystical system or, to borrow an image from architecture, it spans the heights of vision with argumentative buttresses.

When we look back at the whole process, we begin to realize that somewhere between the lyrical revelation of the contemplative state and the mystical commentary on both of them, 'the other side' must have been reached. But as it was the other side of silence, the return to words could not have been easy, either. Perhaps there was another passive journey back, this time not only into the dark night but also into the language of light and shadow, an experience of estrangement which Baudelaire described as passing the forest of symbols.[2]

St. John of the Cross inspires trust because he is so precise in this new-found language. The precision alone suggests that he acts like a traveller returning from the other side, each object, each word has to be known again, for nothing is recognizably familiar. He describes how he exists, burning away with divine love in the darkness to which he had to return. His spirit has been freed from every created thing:

> Mi alma está desasida
> De toda cosa criada—[3]

This freedom must surely extend to the language which can no longer possess him, even when it is ecstatically used, as in '*Coplas . . . sobre un éxtasis de alta contemplación*'. This explains why

---

[1] These are: '*En una nocha oscura*' on which two treatises are based, *Dark Night of the Soul* (*Noche oscura del alma*) and *Ascent of Mount Carmel* (*Subida del monte Carmelo*); *Canciones entre el alma y el Esposo*, which are interpreted in *Spiritual Canticle* (*Cántico espiritual*), and finally the poem '*Oh llama de amor viva*' used in *Living Flame of Love* (*Llama de amor viva*), the shortest of his prose tracts.

[2] In the sonnet '*Correspondances*'. Note, in particular, such phrases as '*à travers des forêts de symboles*', '*dans une ténébreuse et profonde unité*', '*vaste comme la nuit et comme la clarté.*'

[3] '*Glosa a lo divino*'.

some words become reversible in order to be precise, as in the paradox of *arrimo*, support, i.e. being without it in the world of things and yet having it all the time in God, the soul *en su Dios arrimada*.

St. John's poems, whether they describe the return to the night or the journey out of it, must always stay on this side, no matter how strenuous is the desire to hint at the other side through the precision of paradox. Similarly, the illuminated journey, that is the lovebound journey of the spirit, remains enveloped by the dark. There can only be the night journey.

St. John in writing his contemplative verse performed the honest act of skipping over the revealed silence, because he had no language for it.[1] But he firmly acknowledged that the other side of silence was there, beyond the imaginary point of no return. Paradoxically it becomes a point of return once it is reached. Again and again St. John gives his testimony. The best of his poems are beautifully static in their repeated assertions, unlike his prose commentaries; *The Ascent of Mount Carmel*, for instance, elaborates the one basic situation and so achieves a progressive sequence from premise to premise. Here he formulates his distinction between the nights:

> We may say that there are three reasons for which this journey made by the soul to union with God is called night. The first has to do with the point from which the soul goes forth, for it has gradually to deprive itself of desire for all the worldly things which it possessed, by denying them to itself; the which denial and deprivation are, as it were, night to all the senses of man. The second reason has to do with the mean, or the road along which the soul must travel to this union—that is, faith, which is likewise as dark as night to the understanding. The third has to do with the point to which it travels— namely God, who, equally, is dark night to the soul in this life.[2]

The reasons are neatly differentiated and yet kept under one cardinal meaning in a manner similar to the tight interlocking of allegory. One of these reasons reads like a death sentence on poetry. It concerns the night of the senses in which deprivation and denial aim at the roots of imagination. This would certainly

[1] He was, of course, able to turn out devotional verse of the conventional type. His great mystical poems are few.

[2] *Ascent of Mount Carmel*, I, translated by E. Allison Peers, in *The Complete Works of St. John of the Cross* (London, 1953).

destroy any poetic material, if the night journey were meant to stop at the first halt. But St. John's exegesis in prose depends on the continuity of argument, unlike the passivity of mystical union which his poems try to visualize. He maintains the allegorical balance by weighing each premise against God the unknown who 'is dark night to the soul' for the duration of this life.

When he describes ecstasy, it hovers within the depths of solitude (*en profunda soledad*), between the secret wisdom and the dazed unknowing. 'I entered in, I know not where.' And the vocabulary begins to oscillate between the lofty and the very familiar. *Tan embebido*, 'so drunken-reeling' in Roy Campbell's version, is a characteristic phrase. *Balbuciendo*, stammering, goes further in trying to suggest an uncertain state between the known language and the sudden knowledge without understanding (*este saber no sabiendo*).[1]

The paradox of becoming the other person in love was less difficult to express. The Bride and the Bridegroom, *Esposa* and *Esposo*, were familiar representations of the soul united with Christ, and they communicated their joy in passionate dialogue.[2] St. John of the Cross had a Biblical model in the Song of Songs, although it was not a safe text to translate. His great contemporary, Luis de León, learnt this during his troubles with the Inquisition. Pastoral verse, too, influenced the mystical idiom of love. In fact, St. John worked in a rich literary context which must be taken into account, whenever he is judged as a stylist.[3] This does not diminish his originality. On the contrary, it brings out a quality of precision. And this is his own just as stammering is his personal verb of adoration.

One wonders how much his systematic interpretations detach the poems from the aura of the other side, while they succeed in making them clearer to us on this side. Was St. John dissatisfied with poetry? The way in which his prose developed from three lyrical records of ecstasy seems to imply that. A poet's intelli-

---

[1] The quoted examples come from *Coplas . . . sobre un éxtasis de alta contemplación*.

[2] See the '*Canciones entre el alma y el Esposo*', and the commentary on them in *Cántico espiritual*.

[3] The possible influences, however, can be exaggerated. Dámaso Alonso expresses moderate views in *La Poesía de San Juan de la Cruz* (Madrid, 1958), when discussing stylistic analogies with writers like Garcilaso or Sebastián de Córdoba, or with the poetic idiom of the *cancioneros*.

gence is present in his mystical tracts but it is well harnessed to pure discourse. He himself admitted in *Cántico espiritual* (Spiritual Canticle, 1584) that he found current language insufficient for the purpose of explaining mystical poetry.

Do we want to see in St. John of the Cross a mystic in harmony with a poet? I think we do. Yet the image of a disturbed stammerer is nearer to the nature of the poet. St. John, reeling drunk with God, hurls his exclamations into mystical night:

> ¡Oh noche, que guiaste,
> Oh noche amable más que el alborada:
> Oh noche, que juntaste
> Amado con amada,
> Amada en el Amado transformada![1]

The night is still a journey and has one destination for all: death. He who has seen the other side for a glimpse of vision, will always be dying in life. St. John of the Cross expresses the death-wish for all poets: I am dying because I do not die—*Que muero porque no muero*.

2

Matthew Arnold tried to dispose of revealed dogmatic religion by putting high his claims for poetry, and this at a time when verse was everywhere in retreat before the confident advance of the novel. In his essay 'The Study of Poetry' (1880) he wrote:

There is not a creed which is not shaken, not an accredited dogma which is not shown to be questionable, not a received tradition which does not threaten to dissolve. Our religion has materialised itself in the fact, in the supposed fact; it has attached its emotion to the fact, and now the fact is failing it. But for poetry the idea is everything; the rest is a world of illusion, of divine illusion. Poetry attaches its emotion to the idea; the idea *is* the fact. The strongest part of our religion to-day is its unconscious poetry. . . .

More and more mankind will discover that we have to turn to

---

[1] Oh night that was my guide!
  Oh darkness dearer than the morning's pride,
  Oh night that joined the lover
  To the beloved bride
  Transfiguring them each into the other.
The English version is that of Roy Campbell in St. John of the Cross, *Poems*, op. cit. This is the fifth stanza of the famous poem which begins with the line '*En una noche oscura*'.

poetry to interpret life for us, to console us, to sustain us. Without poetry, our science will appear incomplete; and most of what passes with us for religion and philosophy will be replaced by poetry.

Arnold may not be suggesting a complete replacement, nevertheless he assumes that poetry will fare much better during a prolonged crisis of faith than religion; hence his reversal of the priestly function. A muddle in aesthetics is not expected to arise, because his own notions of beauty serve a didactic purpose. In support of this thesis Arnold can safely quote Wordsworth who called poetry 'the breath and finer spirit of all knowledge'. This suits him well, though it is a typical upgrading of the romantic perception.

'But if we conceive thus highly of the destinies of poetry,' Arnold continues, 'we must also set our standard for poetry high.' The trouble with this sort of admonition is that it puts an impossible burden on the poet. If his work, as Arnold seems to imply, is to include a religious quest as well, because a sensitive humanist prefers God to be a tentative metaphor which the poet must find, then the whole business of replacement must precipitate a crisis. Either religion will be lost on the dark journey of style, or the poet will abandon poetry as a religious quest, finding that he is not immune from the mystical predicament of silence.

The Arnold formula, if one can call it that, faces a danger from the practice of poetry rather than of religion, because it is so reversible. It does not take sufficiently into account the mystical current in the poet's imagination which often pulls him towards revelation and dogma, the very things which Arnold hopes to disarm as spiritual authorities. There is a touch of nineteenth-century naïvety in this romantic adulation of fancy with a simultaneous trust in the rational control over it. St. John of the Cross was certainly more sceptical in recognizing the limits of creative imagination. He attached little importance to his verse and would have been astounded to see it used as currency exchangeable for spiritual values. His treatises are a proof of this, particularly the disproportion between the few lines on which he comments and the theological superstructure built upon them.

Arnold for all his lofty ideas came nowhere near the ultimate difficulty of poetic thought. Does it get purer or merely thinner by being elevated? The answer was to be poised obliquely in our own century by Father Bremond who started from a dogmatic position.[1] His intentions, however, were subtle. He felt like many of his contemporaries that too many dregs had settled within the form of poetry, whereas the poetic experience remained inexplicably volatile. A single line could achieve this, for it was not the accumulation or the beauty of words that mattered but 'the mysterious fluid' they were capable of transmitting. In his brave attempt to define what he meant by pure poetry the Abbé Bremond related it to prayer. Within his terms of reference he seemed logical.

The trouble, however, lay deeper and, as with Arnold, concerned the implied replacement. In Bremond's case a prose-infected poem is replaced by a pure poetic state. The analogy with prayer emphasizes the purifying process, 'the Catharsis which is poetry itself', not the external expression. One could, in fact, argue that externalized prayer is bound to be less pure, simply because it has passed through thoughts and words. Pure mental prayer, a state of the soul, needs no image or idea, for there are no ideas that could express the reality called God. Whichever way we look at Bremond's apologia for the essence of poetry, the advocated purity signifies a total dissatisfaction with most elements that have been accepted as poetry. This dissatisfaction makes any process of replacement unworkable. In fact, Bremond rejected so much that he saw words only as '*les magiques intermédiaires*'.

Similar rejection was advocated earlier by E. A. Poe. 'I hold that a long poem does not exist. I maintain that the phrase, "a long poem", is simply a flat contradiction in terms.'[2] It had to rely on prose padding to appear long. A lyrical poem, being short, had at least a chance of remaining pure.

As mental prayer is a state, a passage, so is pure poetry a state and a passage. The night journey applies to them both. For in darkness, as St. John of the Cross tells us, God communicates himself to the soul. When this happens, neither thoughts nor words are capable of being present, even as echoes of silence. A new silence flows from the other side. It is the poet's preroga-

---

[1] Henri Bremond, *La poésie pure* (Abbeville, 1925); *Prière et poésie* (Paris, 1926), translated by Algar Thorold as *Prayer and Poetry* (London, 1927).
[2] *The Poetic Principle*, 1850.

tive to praise the night journey, although at the end of it he finds himself unable to penetrate to the other side.

> Words after speech reach into the silence.[1]

That much the poet can say with full honesty.

3

Silence is the final phase. And it seems to be unavoidable for those who are dissatisfied with poetry while resisting this feeling, as well as for those who, out of the same dissatisfaction, accept the death of poetry. The other side is not a metaphoric reversal. It may be a dark expression, as the night journey is, but it points clearly in one direction. For what comes after silence once it is accepted? A desire for the unknown which cannot be entered. As always when we touch something ultimate we are up against its opposite meaning. Moreover, we want to keep both meanings together under one and the same word. So we need to speak of two silences just as we speak of twin opposites contained in the night journey or in the *noche oscura*.

St. John of the Cross has images of wilful contradiction. One of them is 'luminous darkness'. Faith, too, must be regarded as obscure, because it works beyond our finite intelligence, yet God illuminates this darkness, as in the beginning of creation. *Lux in tenebris lucet.* By comparison with St. John of the Cross Jacob Böhme is a fanciful mystic. St. John's way of *Nada* (nothing) is a delicate spiritual negation. Böhme uses 'No' in a crude and inquisitive manner. Yet he brings off his juxtaposition.[2]

The important thing about opposites like the negative and the positive side of silence is that they create a powerful pull of attraction. We are drawn in before we realize that the unknown has been accepted as unknown. This sensation of being drawn in is like love, it may, in fact, be love itself. No other name need be invoked.

---

[1] T. S. Eliot, *Burnt Norton*, V.

[2] 'Every Divine good power has in the hellish foundation, as in the No, a *contrarium* or opposite, in order that the Yes or the truth may be known. And thus the darkness, as the foundation of God's wrath, has also come into a state of form.' Jacob Böhme, *Quaestiones Theosophicae*, Qu. 8, translated by John Rolleston Earle in *De Electione Gratiae* (London, 1930).

Perhaps the unknown silence is at its closest to poetic truth when mystical opposites become the only language expressing the poet's *via negationis*. Such truth must therefore appear to be negative, this is the *Nada*. It confirms that the poet denies language for ever when he reaches the unknown silence, which is the other side of the silence he has learnt to recognize. Some speak of it in the plural when they mean the companionship of solitude. I go to my solitudes and from my solitudes I come:

> A mis soledades voy,
> De mis soledades vengo.[1]

During the night journey of negation the poet is denied imagination. Its total absence is the darkness in which, however, to use an analogous image to that of St. John, he may sense the luminous silence and be drawn towards it. An ordinary experience of sleeplessness can reveal something of the night's paradoxical dark. It envelops the mind as it obscures the shapes around, yet by intensifying our solitude it becomes a clear dark, a speck of illumination, and lying passively we sometimes feel that other *lux in tenebris*.

Negative appearances tend to confuse us, no matter how firmly we attach them to the idea of opposites. It is easy to confuse the values of experience and knowledge, if their negative meaning is too often stressed. The poet's denial of them may seem like a contempt for knowledge and empirical data. It is true that on occasions the romantic seers behaved as if they despised scientific proof. But there is nothing in the nature of poetry that should automatically set it against the inquiring spirit manifested in knowledge. In commenting on St. John's doctrine of 'unknowing' Thomas Merton distinguishes between man's approach to the universe and his approach to God. All attempts to know God are doomed to fail, for 'there exists no word, no idea that can contain the reality of God'.[2] The sixteenth-century Polish poet Jan Kochanowski used a bold phrase in his hymn to God: 'The Church will not contain you.'[3] 'It is better,

---

[1] Lope de Vega, *La Dorotea*, 1632.
[2] *The Ascent to Truth* (London, 1951), chapter VI. This book discusses the mystical thought of St. John of the Cross.
For a good general essay see Gerald Brenan's 'St. John of the Cross', first published in *Horizon*, vol. XV, and reprinted in Cyril Connolly's anthology *The Golden Horizon* (London, 1953).   [3] '*Kościół cię nie ogarnie*' ('*Pieśń*').

H

here below, to love God than to know him,' we read in a French essay on prayer which is inspired by the teaching of St. Thomas Aquinas (*Melior est amor Dei quam cognitio*).[1]

Such distinctions help us to understand the poetic inquiry and its conflicts. They are caused not so much by other methods of inquiry as by the poet's progress from words to silence. One could, in fact, trace three stages in this progress. At first words predominate, then the poetry of words is drawn to its opposite, silence. Finally, the poetry of silence reveals its own opposite for which there is no word, only the paradoxical other side within the silence. This paradox is similar to the opposite meanings in the mystical night which is both dark and luminous.

In the ultimate analysis the poet's crisis and his experience of silence throw light on his integrity. He cannot evade the challenge. Nor can he delude himself that Word and Silence will be squared in some reality as a reward for accepting the challenge. St. John of the Cross simply rephrased a Biblical quotation to affirm his basic belief:

En el principio moraba
El Verbo, y en Dios vivía . . .[2]

In our times such an appeal to the primal word is reluctantly made, even by poets who have a religious faith. The equation with silence is by no means easy to adopt. But, as a modern Greek poet observes:

The proposition 'In the beginning was the Word' like the geo-metric proposition 'Two parallel lines meet in infinity' proves nothing but itself. It is a principle on which to construct a geometry or a religion. . . . A metaphysic is an imaginary line dividing an invisible territory. The division enables us to measure the territory and to determine our own position in it. A compass with which human beings are supplied from birth.[3]

4

The twentieth century is intensely dark and intensely luminous. The paradox of the night journey still applies to the prospects

[1] Jacques and Raïssa Maritain, *Prayer and Intelligence*, translated by Algar Thorold (London, 1928).

[2] '*Sobre el Evangelio "In principio erat Verbum"* '.

[3] Nanos Valaoritis, 'Problems of an Empire' in *Botteghe Oscure*, vol. XX (Autumn 1957).

which this age offers. Besides, the speed of the journey is most impressive if we watch the technological scenery passing by. And there are moments when the acquisition of knowledge gives us a feeling that we are close to the truth. Why then should the final mystery remain at the same elusive distance?

The distance has always been elusive because it grows in relation to the increase of knowledge and its complexity. Again and again we are reminded of the impossibility of solving the mystery and this gnaws at our death-bound existence. Is God this mystery, or is it the distance to him that deludes us? The question seems wide open and the truth as intangible as the other side of silence. A few weeks before his death Yeats wrote in a letter:

It seems to me that I have found what I wanted. When I try to put all into a phrase I say, 'Man can embody truth but he cannot know it.' I must embody it in the completion of my life. The abstract is not life and everywhere draws out its contradictions.[1]

No abstractions, no bookish activity, for 'it is more difficult to live in goodness through a single day than to write a book'.[2] Mickiewicz put this thought into an epigram, one of several inspired by Jacob Böhme, Angelus Silesius, and Saint-Martin, his favourite trinity of mystics. In a letter to a friend he was even more explicit: 'It seems to me that the time will come when it will be necessary to become a saint in order to become a poet.'[3] This is an illuminist setting up an ideal higher than that of genius.

But few among Christian saints and among the holy men in the East had the desire to express themselves in poetry. St. Francis of Assisi and St. John of the Cross wrote verse of great distinction, yet they preferred to explore contemplative silence. Both, however, kept their poetic grace. St. Francis, in particular, showed it in his actions which were, like parables, charged with imagination. True to the poetry of his age, he was a troubadour of holiness who praised his Lady Poverty.

---

[1] To Lady Elizabeth Pelham, 4 January 1939. *The Letters of W. B. Yeats*, edited by Allan Wade (London, 1954).

[2] W słowach tylko chęć widzim, w działaniu potęgę,
Trudniej dzień dobrze przeżyć, niż napisać księgę.
('*Słowo i czyn*')

[3] To H. Kajsiewicz, 31 October 1835.

St. John experienced the other side. Because of this, the *noche oscura* was always present in his life. It is said that he would sit in a small dark place, and through a window contemplate a distant landscape. His eyes, I feel, were fixed on the other side of silence.

CHAPTER XI

THE FAILURE OF MYSTICAL VERSE

I

St. John of the Cross was almost unique in giving his mystical experience a poetic form which somehow still convinces. Apart from commenting on his poems, in copious prose and at a later date, he wrote nothing else. As a poet he was in the literal sense single-minded, his inner eye had only one object in view. He admitted no intrusion from the senses, although he loved the beauty, *toda la hermosura*, of the external world. Many poets have at one time or another attempted a mystical subject, but because this was occasional writing it had to remain unrelated to their experience as a whole, proving what the poets wanted perhaps to prove to themselves: that the record of mystical experience was as much a freak as the experience itself. In a sense they hardly differed from those contributors to anthologies who write on the theme 'I also had a mystical experience'. One cannot imagine St. John polluting the poetic idiom he had discovered for his experience with any other subject afterwards. The purity of the words he used had to be permanent. A believer who accepts his sainthood would, no doubt, ascribe a sacramental quality to St. John's verse.

Without this quality, whether it is accepted or not, most mystical writing seems to be unsatisfactory. The failure may not be obvious at first to contemporaries, but with time the vocabulary shows up its weakness. The wrong precision or the abstract vagueness will be noticed sooner or later. And fashion too, whether baroque or romantic in style, tends to destroy the uniqueness of experience which for a mystical record is essential. This, of course, becomes clearer with the passage of time.

The mystical has unintentionally acquired the appeal of something bizarre rather than rare or difficult to attain. Richard Crashaw in his baroque praise of 'the Admirable Sainte Teresa', tells us how eager she was to renounce the terrestrial semblances of love:

> Farewell then, all the world! Adieu.
> Teresa is no more for you.
> Farewell, all pleasures, sports, and ioyes,
> (Never till now esteemed toyes)
> Farewell that ever deare may be
> Mother's armes or Father's knee.
> Farewell house, and farewell home!
> She's for the Moores, and Martyrdom.

There is, no doubt, charm in such innocence of a saint to be, which the poet himself mocks with a colloquial exclamation:

> Sweet, not so fast! lo thy fair Spouse
> Whom thou seekst with so swift vowes,
> Calls thee back . . .[1]

Yet the poem as a whole fails to convince one of its mystical subject, partly because it is mounted in the panegyrical manner of the age, and partly because its figures of speech seem to intensify the freakish aspect of holiness.

Another seventeenth-century poet, Thomas Traherne, concentrates more on the preparative phase of mysticism and can therefore restrict himself to momentary states, thus achieving greater precision than Crashaw. 'Flight is but the preparative', he says in 'The Vision' and devotes a poem to the theme of Anticipation, which opens with this statement:

> My contemplation dazzles in the End
> Of all I comprehend . . .

It has this in common with the beginning of Vaughan's 'The World' ('I saw Eternity the other night/Like a great *Ring* of pure and endless light'), that the initial statement lifts our imagination at once to a very high plane, but in neither poem do the stanzas that follow fulfil the expectations raised; on the contrary, we are made to descend step by step, down the familiar ladder of conceits.

In 'The Anticipation', Traherne elaborates the meaning of the End in relation to Him whose 'Essence is all Act'. The poem is neatly summed up as the conceptual manner requires:

> He is the means of both Himself and all,
> Whom we the Fountain, Means and End do call.

[1] 'A Hymn to the Name and Honor of the Admirable Sainte Teresa.'

In 'The World', Vaughan proceeds to illustrate the contrast between the Ring of Eternity and the World of Time in it, with the stock examples of 'the doting Lover', 'the darksome States-man', 'the fearfull miser', and so on. I do not think that the conceptual method goes well with the moment of vision recorded in the first two lines: very little has in fact been added to them, despite the lengthy stanzas.

Crashaw at least succeeds in creating the mood of rapture in the St. Teresa poem by his display of rhetoric. 'O how oft', 'How kindly', 'O what delight'—the poem races on and at the end 'thousands of crown'd Soules', who throng to be themselves Teresa's crown, do achieve the effect of a magnificent spiritual congestion. Crashaw certainly indulges in metaphysical freaks, but he has no desire to explain them away in a steady argument.

Wherever a conceit merges poetically with an argument, it is achieved at each point by the basic simile which is strong enough to receive a mystical charge. Andrew Marvell's 'On a Drop of Dew' possesses this quality. Superficially, it resembles other conceptual poems in its distribution of parallel attributes (the soul is that drop of dew), but the wonder is there at each successive meeting point. The little globe, the great heaven in an heaven less, the manna's sacred dew are all poetically distilled from a substance so rich that it seems to vouch for a mystical experience.

Marvell's precision, too, inspires trust in the poem. Unlike the Romantics and their successors he does not exceed the function of detail. He knows which attributes of the drop of dew are relevant to his idea of the soul, but he is not being descriptive, either for the sake of a natural phenomenon or for the sake of conceit.

2

Excessive description is often fatal to mystical writing; it increases the atmosphere of mere freakishness. The nineteenth century, with its interest in mesmerism and experimental mediumship, favoured the tricks which could make the mystery visible. The supernatural, the mystical, and the weird had to be described, preferably in great detail, so that the freakish would become familiar:

> We vibrate to the pant and thrill
>> Wherewith Eternity has curled
> In serpent-twine about God's seat;
> While, freshening upward to His feet
> In gradual growth His full-leaved will
> Expands from world to world.[1]

Even Tennyson has to rely on natural trappings to endow Sir Galahad's holy pursuit with visible signs. These show that he is trotting on the right track, after all:

> The clouds are broken in the sky,
>> And thro' the mountain-walls
> A rolling organ-harmony
>> Swells up, and shakes and falls.
> Then move the trees, the copses nod,
>> Wings flutter, voices hover clear:
> 'O just and faithful knight of God!
>> Ride! the prize is near.'[2]

This is straightforward stuff, descriptive for a purpose. It can easily become interchangeable with abstract correspondences, and the road to symbolism is open. Then a real brook means the symbolic brook, and of course a rose is inevitably, as always, the Rose.

In earlier pre-Romantic symbolism the interchangeable mystical values have a more intriguing quality, as for instance in Blake's poems, but the danger there seems to lie in the very flux of correspondences. To take a most obvious example: would Blake's mystical intention be radically altered if he had asked the reader to see a Heaven in a grain of sand (instead of a World) and a World in a wild flower?[3] Likewise, in the next equation, could not Eternity be held in the palm of the hand? Perhaps the fascination which Blake's poetry exercises depends to some degree on our willingness to accept such flexible links. There is truly a spontaneous innocence in the way his words seek one another's company. The symbolist of a later date would be stricter with his correspondences, but as a result far less surprising.

Description may be clogged with detail, but a good poet can

---

[1] Elizabeth Barrett Browning, 'Human Life's Mystery', stanza 3.
[2] 'Sir Galahad', final stanza.
[3] 'Auguries of Innocence'.

avoid this danger, and nevertheless opt for the concrete detail rather than allow huge abstractions to take over. The grandeur of God in the world flames out for Hopkins like 'shining from shook foil'. The foil is particular, and so is the lightning effect; he stresses their specific connotation in a letter.[1] When Rilke unfolds his final map of existence in the Tenth Duino Elegy, he has again to particularize, even to name, although the names of his places belong to the geography of allegory. The Hills of Primeval Suffering, *die Berge des Urleids*, for example, stand out clear in his panorama; the mystical clings desperately to the visible.

Eliot pins down his mystical poems to concrete spots in real geography, each of his *Four Quartets* takes its name from an existing place. *East Coker*, for instance, is a village in Somerset, *The Dry Salvages* is a small group of rocks off the coast of Massachusetts. Yet there is something elusive about all those titles. *Burnt Norton* is a deserted manor house with a garden—and Eliot once wandered into it, that much we know; but the gate, the empty alley, and the drained pool are made strangely placeless in the poem.

Whatever is done to and with objects in the descriptive transference, there cannot be, we feel, a fixed system in mystical writing, anything resembling the spheres, whether of knowledge or intuition. Blake therefore had everything to gain from his provisional symbols. Even when he asserted the truth as revealed to him (e.g. in *The Marriage of Heaven and Hell*) he managed to suggest that it was a provisional revelation. He remained a cautionary mystic to the end, from *Songs of Innocence* to *Milton*, despite the rambling noise of his prophetic verbiage. Once his ideas began to work for those who read him in another century, they also provided a suggestion that the failure of mystical verse should perhaps be regarded as provisional. If this holds for Blake, it can surely hold for other poets, or at least some of them, who are for a time under the cloud of their own language. The English Metaphysicals were invisible for over two centuries, until the baroque style no longer proved a hindrance to perception.

With his acute poetic self-perception Walt Whitman could now and again see right through language and disperse a cloud

---

[1] 'I mean foil in its sense of leaf or tinsel. . . . Shaken goldfoil gives off broad glares like sheet lightning' (to Robert Bridges, 4 January 1883). See *Poems of Gerard Manley Hopkins*, 4th ed. (London, 1967), note to 'God's Grandeur', p. 263.

before it gathered round his words. For he meant words as well when he spoke about the inclusive nature of truth:

> Meditating among liars, and retreating sternly into myself, I see
> that there are really no liars or lies after all,
> And nothing fails its perfect return—And that what are called
> lies are perfect returns,
> And that each thing exactly represents itself, and what has pre-
> ceded it,
> And that the truth includes all, and is compact, just as much as
> space is compact,
> And that there is no law or vacuum in the amount of the truth—
> but that all is truth without exception;
> And henceforth I will go celebrate anything I see or am,
> And sing and laugh, and deny nothing.

This makes sense, good common sense, in relation to words, and because Whitman is here both colloquial and personal, his voice seems all the more sincere against the background of mystical rhetorics and revelations. None of his abstractions, and there are many, sounds hollow: this is certainly a stylistic achievement. When compared with most poems included in *The Oxford Book of English Mystical Verse*, Whitman's 'All is Truth' gains in appearing to be a poem possessed by the sense of revelation whilst the others often give the impression of conventional sameness. On second reading, however, one may be inclined to accept Whitman's excellence in terms of a statement. Not quite a manifesto, but most certainly a declaration. And it turns out to be primarily applicable to Whitman's method. As a declaration it must stand alone, for it cannot be repeated. This is its strength and also its limitation. A minor imitative poet would not be able to get far ahead with Whitman's inclusive credo. Denying nothing could so very easily lead to a sort of *laissez-faire*, a happy-go-lucky celebration of anything.

There exists, after all, much devotional writing in which the celebration of God in anything has resulted in a facile heightening of tone which differs little from the panegyrical abuses of the baroque and Augustan poetasters. In a curious and paradoxical way then, Whitman's sensible reminder that All is Truth points to the very area where mystical verse fails most frequently. By accepting all experience it blears the meaning of the unique experience. The failure lurks somewhere between the commendable principle of acceptance and the equally necessary art of discrimination. The mystical embrace of things is not as easy as the desire for it would seem to suggest.

On a theological level the same difficulty presents itself, although we expect the language to be more formal and stricter in the use of terms. When a very original voice attracts attention, as that of Nicholas of Cusa, a fifteenth-century cardinal and mystic, it speaks from an experience which we want to imagine. Dr. Happold in his admirably lucid books on mysticism[1] accords Nicholas of Cusa a special place. His is the mind which prefigures many diverse minds: those of poets like Blake, Whitman, or Eliot, of thinkers like Schopenhauer and Jung. Here is a quotation from Nicholas of Cusa, a quotation which Dr. Happold rightly considers to be relevant to our way of thinking in this age, which explores space and the psyche:

> Hence I observed how needful it is for me to enter into the darkness, and to admit the coincidence of opposites, beyond all the grasp of reason, and there to seek the truth where impossibility meeteth me.[2]

The idea of the reconcilable opposites is the same as the *coniunctio oppositorum* of the alchemists, to which Jung often returns in his final essays.[3] Acceptance means sanity, and reconciliation within a paradox brings us near to our true undivided selves. But does it all translate into the language of poetry, especially when used for a mystical purpose? Nicholas of Cusa appeals to the imagination. But can his image of the ultimate reality, which is both within grasp and beyond description, ever serve the poet whose job it is to reach out with words towards the unimaginable and to glimpse thoughts in their constant transmutation if only for one visible moment? Failure seems to be a frequent result.

3

Yet there is something positive and meaningful about such a failure. Mystical verse may, in fact, show the way to the negative

---

[1] F. C. Happold, *Mysticism* (London, 1964). See also *Religious Faith and Twentieth-Century Man* (London, 1966).

[2] *De Visione Dei*, translated by E. G. Salter as *The Vision of God* (London, 1928).

[3] E.g. 'Late Thoughts', in *Memories, Dreams, Reflections* (London, 1963). Cf. Blake's 'Without contraries there is no progression' (*The Marriage of Heaven and Hell*).

or positive acceptance of failure. What often happens is this: realizing that the silence behind words must have a purpose, the poet decides to stop at this point. This is his negative acceptance of failure. Should he, however, desire to explore the other side of silence, his acceptance would be positive, but in the same difficult sense that the mystic's acceptance is positive when he merely exercises his spiritual faculties. The practitioner of verse has come close to the practitioner of spiritual silence, and at this moment his understanding of language needs no words to express the understanding. The paradox has turned round on itself.

I have partially discussed this paradox in the chapter on language as experience, in which my argument rests on the poets' repeated claim throughout the ages that they invest language with their own immortality. But, as I have tried to show, the experience of oneself in language puts higher and higher demands on both sincerity and the art of precision. This produces tension and eventually results in a crisis.

Thomas Merton has observed in *The Ascent to Truth* that:

The experience of the artist and the experience of the mystic are completely different. Although it is quite possible for a man to be both an artist and a mystic at the same time, his art and his mysticism must always remain two essentially different things. . . . The only true mysticism is religious mysticism (chapter IV).

Elsewhere he has written that 'a bad book about the love of God remains a bad book, even though it may be about the love of God'.[1]

Merton died in 1968. As a Trappist he had been, first of all, a practitioner of silence, but he was also a writer, and very successful by the standards accepted outside his seclusion. I hope it is not presumptuous on my part to assume that he was until his death searching for the other side of silence. The objective is the same for all mystics, whether they are in the stage of eloquence or in one of the stages of silence.

We read Thomas Merton with curiosity because in this age of immediate and instant documentation we want to partake of other people's experience, almost as it is happening to them. A man who has conquered Mount Everest, circled the globe in a *sputnik*, or walked in space, differs from the champions of the

[1] *The Sign of Jonas* (London, 1953).

past because he has become a recorded, verifiable myth; he confirms our own present with his exploits which can be looked up at will on a screen and heard on a tape. Each verification is a reassuring proof to the senses of our reality.

We tend, I think, to treat past exploits in a similar way, looking for bits of documentation. St. John of the Cross fascinates, not unlike a champion, a conqueror who emerged on the other side of the *noche oscura* and was awarded the halo of sainthood by his Church. As for his poetry, it seems to possess that verifiable quality which our age approves of. After all, the saint himself regarded his verse as a document to be commented upon, and accordingly he built a theological superstructure, an imposing glossary which has undoubtedly made the interpretation of the poems much easier for his future readers.

We have in St. John of the Cross a poet, a theologian, and a critic, and the combination is today bound to impress those who may scorn mysticism, but respect introspection. Perhaps there is a lesson in this posthumous success for poets who are ready to climb the mystical heights simply because, like Mount Everest, they are there. The lesson is hard if it means a challenge of experience so great that it can only be fulfilled in a verifiable myth. For the poet-mystic it amounts to the challenge of sainthood. Nothing less will do. Since so much mystical verse fails to satisfy as poetry, the modern man is inclined to believe that it has no value as a record. There is hardly any point in trying to verify it against the man's life.

Holiness then may be the magnetic force which attracts the poet to the other side of silence.

> In a valey of this restless minde
> I soughte in mounteine and in mede,
> Trustinge a trewe love for to finde.
> Upon an hill than I took hede;
> A voice I herde, and neer I yede,
> In huge doulour complaininge tho,
> See, derè soule, how my sides blede,
> *Quia amore langueo.*[1]

The voice is Christ's, speaking to the human soul. It speaks in a fifteenth-century poem which is anonymous; no personal

[1] '*Quia amore langueo*'; the text as in *Early English Lyrics*, chosen by E. K. Chambers and F. Sidgwick (London, 1947).

voice mediates and this certainly adds to the impact of the words. The further we go into the past, the more this anonymity of mystical voices suggests to us that the personal, the I, is taken over, as it should be, by the other presence. We feel nearer to it than we do in the modern idiom which would be more easily understood, but therefore charged with our personal associations. When we read the medieval complaints of Christ or the Virgin Mary, with the cross *arbor una nobilis*,[1] we feel that the anonymous writer wants us to participate in that other voice. And we know he believes in the possibility of the participation as Dante believed in the Theocentric system with Purgatory, Hell, and Heaven as its ultimate realities. Because of this assumed participation, the Virgin Mary under the Cross speaks in the present, within the undivided time which holds the Annunciation and the Passion in the same scales, and we are the witnesses:

> Oh, angel Gabriel
> where is that range of joy
> you promised me would never change?
> You said: 'Virgin, you are filled with love',
> but now I am full of a great grief.
> My body has rotted inside me and my bones moulder.
> Oh, all you wistful mothers, implore God
> that such a sight may never visit your children,
> not this which I, a poor woman, now witness.[2]

4

In the Old Testament the voice of God is often heard, but the participation there cannot be of the same directness as with Christ, nor is it assumed to be so. The early image of the Deity, particularly in the Book of Job, strikes the modern man as difficult to accept. Job we feel was unfairly treated, he had no chance whatsoever to establish a relationship with his Maker. This modern objection prompted Jung to write a separate study in defence of the poor faithful Job.[3]

---

[1] From the hymn, *'Pange lingua gloriosi'*, by Fortunatus, sixth century.

[2] 'Lament of Our Lady under the Cross' (*Żale Matki Boskiej pod Krzyżem*), a fifteenth-century poem, from *Five Centuries of Polish Poetry*, op. cit.

[3] *Antwort auf Hiob* (1952), translated as *Answer to Job* (London, 1954). 'Yahweh's intention to become man, which resulted from his collision with Job, is fulfilled in Christ's life and suffering' (VII).

The mystical implications, however, are less righteous, for the story is singularly free from childish naïvety about heavenly paternalism. Job is presented *sub specie aeternitatis*, a small existence within the pattern of good and evil, where the forces of creation are being balanced, one against the other. The experience of such a total view was for Job threatening at first as for a mystic, then dazzling within the presence of God who chose to give his total inclusive answers. The mystical voice is here God's voice and man is the listener. The holiness lies within this humility of being a listener.

The trouble with mystical poetry of the impressionistic kind is the direction of its voice—from man to God, the latter assumed to be a listener, and not the other way round. The total view from this level must therefore be impossible to place into focus, let alone describe.

Instead, the poet reaches out with abstract words towards the abstractions which he attributes to the Deity. A fourth-century hymn, written by St. Ambrose, the Bishop of Milan, begins with these words:

> Splendor paternae gloriae,
> de luce lucem proferens,
> lux lucis et fons luminis,
> dies dierum illuminans . . .[1]

The Latin sounds sonorous and there is reverence in the repeated idea of light. But the abstract canker sets in. Later it seems almost hereditary in most devotional writing. Poet after poet gropes in the morass of pious sentiments, fondles the image of holiness as if it were a precious archetypal find; he murmurs reverently, intones or bellows in a dim religious light of his own manufacture. His is the *noche oscura* full of noises, of words being hit and stumbled over.

He could at any moment do otherwise, let go of the mystical soliloquy and *ad maiorem Dei gloriam* keep mum.

[1] *The Oxford Book of Medieval Latin Verse*, edited by F. J. E. Raby (Oxford, 1959).

CHAPTER XII

THE SWALLOW ON THE SUNDIAL

I

At noon on Sunday the fifth of September, 1965, I happened to walk into St. Damian's church outside Assisi just as a special mass was about to be celebrated, during which I was to hear St. Francis's 'Canticle of Brother Sun' chanted by the monks. St. Francis had received his vocation at this church which was to become a convent of Poor Clares. And it was here, in a minute terrace garden, that years later, during a convalescence, blind, he composed his song of praise which I was now given the chance to hear in its precise setting.

The well inside the cloister served as an altar, and the fruits of the season were brought in and placed on the altar. And then the Franciscan monks went round, under the cloister arches, chanting the verses in their saint's vernacular. The sun stood high, the air seemed to breathe out light, and swallows started swooping into the blue square of the sky above our heads.

Nothing could have been more spontaneously harmonious than this display of the poetic words illustrated, moment after moment, by the living creation. No religious commitment was necessary. The occasion had everything to offer. A student of mythology or comparative religion, a Jungian or Freudian psychologist would have been satisfied by the combined symbol of the well and the altar, by the fruit sacrifice and the sun giving its benign blessing.

But since so little can escape recording in the twentieth century, there were cameras, both pious and commercial, clicking between the pillars, and a television monster eyed the details of the scene, each take supervised efficiently by a priest. There was a Nordic lady, too, armed with a portable arsenal of photographic gadgets, who would from time to time jump into the centre where the priests stood, let her apparatus click and rustle before she was gently removed from the forbidden area. And the swallows kept their swooping survey of the cloister. Finally, I myself succumbed to the recording temptation when

I looked at the wall opposite and saw that one of the swallows had landed on the sundial and was sitting there gracefully, propped almost at the tip of the gnomon. It remained quite still, unconcerned by my snapshot.

A few weeks later I had the prints developed in London. The eye of my camera had captured it all, the cloister garden of St. Damian with its well, sundial, all except the swallow. I looked through a magnifying glass, examined every detail. Yes, there was the metal rod, even the numbers on the sundial were visible. But not that most appropriate visitor which had descended from the sky so poetically.

Whose fault it could have been no longer mattered. I had failed to record the swallow on the sundial: this was the fact and it had, for me at least, some significance as a failure in what I would call a presumptuous groping for a mystical event. The record remained in the inner eye, more vivid perhaps than any possible snapshot, yet to the outside world of documentators and verifiers there was no proof. A sympathetic listener might probably grant me some poetic licence, a mystical metaphor at the most; others would very likely mark me in their minds as a harmless liar.

A personal significance, however, persists, because the swallow on the dial has within this unified image a *coniunctio oppositorum*: swiftness and stillness, time reduced to the pinhead of a moment, the sun and the shadow on the dial. More contrasts could be found to add to the pattern. In relation to the problems discussed throughout this book, the image seems to stand for their ultimate conjunction as the other side of silence becomes the poet's fulfilment, acceptable, though beyond the reach of words. The swallow, too, placed itself on the visible point of time, or so it seemed, but it eluded the possible permanence of a pictorial record; it was, in fact, unreachable, on the other side of the image.

One believes in both sides of silence during a visit to Assisi; the contemplative air of the place belongs to each individual moment of experience and is, above all, permeated with the saint's presence. The words he put together at St. Damian's in such early vernacular, are verifiable in a sense that is possible with few poems. They speak about my lord Brother Sun and the light we are given through him, about Brother Wind and

I

Sister Water which is humble, precious, and pure, about Brother Fire and Sister Earth, our mother, and the mother of herbs and fruits with coloured flowers.

> Laudatu sie, mi signore, cum tucte le tue creature,
>   Spetialmente messor lo frate sole,
>   Lo qual è jorno el allumini noi per lui. . . .
>
> Laudato si', mi signore, per frate vento,
>   Et per aere et nubilo et sereno et onne tempo,
>   Per lo quale a le tue creature dài sustentamento.
> Laudatu si', mi signore, per sor aqua,
>   La quale è multo utile et humile et pretiosa et casta.
> Laudatu si', mi signore, per frate focu . . .
> . . . .
> Laudatu si', mi signore, per sora nostra matre terra,
>   La quale ne sustenta et governa,
>   Et produce diversi fructi con coloriti flori et herba.[1]

This *laudes creaturarum*, a hymn of praise through all the things made by God, is rooted in contemplative silence. It may not appeal to modern readers, but no sceptic today can question the sincerity of the man who called the sun his brother. Joseph Conrad used the example of St. Francis when he wanted to defend patriotism against fashionable scoffing:

patriotism—a somewhat discredited sentiment, because the delicacy of our humanitarians regards it as a relic of barbarism. Yet neither the great Florentine painter who closed his eyes in death thinking of his city, nor St. Francis, blessing with his last breath the town of Assisi, were barbarians.[2]

St. Francis was no phoney cosmopolitan, nor had his mystic probing into silence any resemblance to Pascal's intellectual awe at the silence of the infinite spaces. Like a true poet, he feared the delusion and the vanity of abstractions. That is why even the most extravagant tales recorded by his admirers emphasize the saint's love of the concrete. A wolf, a swallow, a lark, a rock on Mount La Verna—these were objects touched with his attentive respect. For this reason his contemporaries

[1] I have used the most easily available version as given in *The Oxford Book of Italian Verse* (1952 ed.). The canticle is known by a number of traditional titles, both Latin and Italian, e.g. '*Laudes creaturarum*', '*Cantico delle creature*', '*Canticum fratris solis*', '*Cantico di frate Sole*'. A recent critical study of both the sources and the text is Vittore Branca's '*Il Cantico di Frate Sole*' in *Archivum Franciscanum Historicum*, vol. XLI (November 1949).   [2] *Prince Roman.*

felt it their duty to recapture and pass on to posterity the physical features of the man from Assisi.

The painter Cimabue managed to draw the tormented and resigned humanity of the saint. He showed us the face we believe to be true, unlike the glossy prettiness of youth in St. Antony's portraits which hardly correspond to the reality of the bald and corpulent saint. The difference between the concrete and the mythical is well contrasted in the two men who, after all, belonged to the same age and the same religious order. In St. Francis's case the difference emphasizes not only his historical reality but also his actual presence, sensed in the city of Assisi and the serene landscape of Umbria.

St. Francis succeeded, as perhaps no other saint did, in emulating the human ideal in Christ, and because of it, like Christ, he has to be experienced in the present. His historical meaning is of secondary importance.

2

Now the question of being truly in the present concerns the mystic as much as the poet, and over this they both stumble in their search for illuminated silence on the other side of death-wishes, despair, sacrifice, and failure.

The poet-prophet deludes himself by trying to trace the contours of the future in the events which mask the present for him; the poet-activist bangs the surface of what is contemporary, hoping to impress himself on the days before they vanish in the noise he is making. Neither the physical suicide nor the suicidal sacrifice of one's art can damage the instinct of self-preservation which maintains life at large. Schopenhauer reminds us that life's own assurance is the will to live and that it has no other form but the continuous present.[1] It was this awareness that brought Schopenhauer to the doors of mystical perception.

[1]   In der Vergangenheit hat kein Mensch gelebt, und in der Zukunft wird nie einer leben; sondern die Gegenwart allein is die Form alles Lebens, ist aber auch sein sicherer Besitz, der ihm nie entrissen werden kann. . . .

Die Gegenwart allein ist Das, was immer da ist und unverrückbar feststeht. Empirisch aufgefasst das Flüchtigste von Allem, stellt sie dem metaphysischen Blick, der über die Formen der empirischen Anschauung hinwegsieht, sich als das allein Beharrende dar, das *Nunc Stans* der Scholastiker.
                Die Welt als Wille und Vorstellung, vol. I, book IV, §54.

Kierkegaard tells us that 'The poet is the child of eternity, but he lacks the seriousness of eternity'.[1] Coleridge, on the other hand, wants the poet to be that which he himself aspired to be: 'No man was ever yet a great poet without being at the same time a profound philosopher.'[2] Whether a philosopher or a child of eternity, the poet is confined to the present, of which he must have a heightened awareness in order to remain a poet. But like any human being he cannot bear the present as a continuous flow of events, and prefers to lock himself up in a pattern of time. 'We are all serving a life sentence in the dungeon of self.'[3] Instead of being opened out, the psyche suffers from the claustrophobia of time with the past and the future closing in and always shifting their barriers.

Time defines man's existential paradox. He is living in the present without, in fact, seeing the real present whose other name is eternity. Unless 'you become as little children, you shall not enter into the kingdom of heaven'.[4] Children live in the present. Christ alluded to the eternity of the continuous present which the child's mind totally accepts and then loses. The poet does not leap over death as Coleridge would have us believe, but he does leap over moments in the continuous present which he senses in a manner not unlike that of children. Wordsworth expressed this affinity with childhood when he wrote about the intimations of immortality.

The poet then must live in the real present and accept his childlike condition. He may lack the seriousness of eternity about which Kierkegaard speaks, and he may not be one of the little children for whom Christ keeps his kingdom of heaven open. Yet, now more than ever, he has to meet the challenge of the age in the obvious manifestations of the present. They have already affected his range of vision. For the twentieth century is language-conscious, preoccupied with semantics, etymologies, and comparative linguistics. Words are not only studied as entities, but placed again and again in relative contexts; even the verbal ambiguities of poetry seem to be resolvable in the light of their own obscurity.

[1] 'The lilies of the field and the birds of the air', op. cit.
[2] *Biographia Literaria*, chapter 15.
[3] Cyril Connolly ('Palinurus'), *The Unquiet Grave* (London, 1945).
[4] Matthew, 18.

If so much is really known of language as a tool, if all tools are easily manufactured, the poet may well ask himself whether he is becoming redundant, just like some archaic artisan or a tramp tinker, his workshop even smaller than a pack. Perhaps in the end there will be no Word. And what is to remain of meaning? Perhaps some microscopic phonemes of utterance, each recordable, each automatically segregated from its original impulse.

As for the range of the poet's vision, the challenge today comes from space. This is, in fact, a vast vision, being realized in our presence: the workshop of imagination shows its finished products. These are not poetic imaginings, huge cloudy symbols of a high romance, stars invoked in nebulous epithets: even the much apostrophized moon after centuries of lyrical ebb and flow has suddenly become tangible. Should the popular fantasies of Outer Space be now considered as the subject of poetry? Or the mountains of the Moon? In the eighteenth century, the age of reason, Collins wrote an ode on 'the Popular Superstitions of the Highlands of Scotland considered as the subject of poetry'.

Whatever the new-found Space may do to the poet's imagination and reason, it will certainly open more mystical queries. Here lies the challenge and also the trap. For when the barrier of silence is reached as definitely as it is now, no exclamatory protestations, no wooing of death can release the poet from the apprehension that silence is a clear line on the map of poetry. There may be no words beyond the line, but the absence of words need not mean their death. Perhaps silence stands for survival.

One of the new mystical queries concerns, I think, the affinity between the silence of space at last experienced by man, and the silence within him, into which, as into a prehistoric cave, depth psychology probes, searching for the light on the other side. Myth can be a guide to the past-present, if one wants to see the two unified, but can it still serve as a mediator in the vertical relationship with the cosmic areas outside our global awareness which is bound to shrink anyway, as the other awareness takes possession of our minds.

To fall back on any universal pattern of the past would be useless. We can no longer lift up the Chestertonian banner of chivalry: back to the Middle Ages, to the Gothic arches and the dim religious light of stained-glass windows. Nor would we find aesthetic comfort, however small, in some kind of Pre-Raphaelite revival. The weakness of mystical verse and painting in the nineteenth century was precisely the revivalist tone, the mawkish affirmation which went together with the simultaneous denial of the real present. The pretty Italian features of Christ in devotional pictures were as irrelevant as the genteel raptures over some unearthly beatitude. When Dante wrote that love moved the sun and the other stars, he was also stating a fact which theocentric science accepted; those who tried to imitate Dante in the nineteenth century could with luck revive the mood but not the science. The intention went awry.

Today the poet has more than ever to exercise the two faculties at his disposal: intuition and imagination. Both bring him close to the frontier of words and he learns from the first experience of silence that the real present cannot be entered unless it is reached through silence. The crisis, the sacrifice, and the *noche oscura* occur in the same vertical relationship with that other silence, at which the poet hurls his questions, supplications, and abuse. He is never answered, although like Job he believes in the Voice on the inscrutable side of silence.

Turning inwards, however, he might find that other side in himself. Perhaps then, and only then, would he astonish his own poetic desire by feeling no need of a voice. All is answered in the negative. Schopenhauer understood mysticism when he said that his system on reaching its highest point ended with a negation.[1]

A swallow perched on the gnomon of a sundial balances a paradox over the shadow line which indicates a small measure of time. The line could be extinguished at any moment by the withdrawal of light or by the swallow's own shadow. But the swallow prefers to be uncapturable, and withdraws into measureless light.

Assisi 1965—*Vienna* 1967

---

[1] 'Diesem nun entspricht es, dass meine Lehre, wenn auf ihrem Gipfelpunkt angelangt, einen *negativen* Charakter annimmt, also mit einer Negation endigt.' *Die Welt als Wille und Vorstellung*, vol. II, Book IV, chapter 48.

INDEX OF NAMES

Passages dealing in some detail with the following
are indicated by bold-face references.